AI Changing the Arc of Educational Leadership

Karen Moran Jackson • Rosemary Papa

AI Changing the Arc of Educational Leadership

palgrave
macmillan

Karen Moran Jackson (iD)
Soka University of America
Aliso Viejo, CA, USA

Rosemary Papa
Emerita, Professor Educational
Leadership and The Dale & Jewell
Lewis Endowed Chair, Learning
Centered Leadership
Northern Arizona University
Flagstaff, AZ, USA

ISBN 978-3-031-71414-6   ISBN 978-3-031-71415-3   (eBook)
https://doi.org/10.1007/978-3-031-71415-3

This Palgrave Macmillan imprint is published by the registered company Springer Nature Switzerland AG.
The registered company address is: Gewerbestrasse 11, 6330 Cham, Switzerland

If disposing of this product, please recycle the paper.

FOREWORD

As the Superintendent of a diverse and dynamic school district, I have witnessed firsthand the transformative power of technology in education. The rapid advancements in Artificial Intelligence (AI) have ushered in a new era, presenting unprecedented opportunities and significant challenges for educational leaders. Within this context, "AI Changing the Arc of Educational Leadership" by Karen Moran Jackson and Rosemary Papa emerges as a crucial and timely contribution to the discourse on educational innovation.

This book explores AI in Education (AIED), dissecting its multifaceted impact on the educational landscape. Jackson and Papa meticulously analyze how AI is reshaping the roles of students, teachers, educational leaders, and parents. Their work is a theoretical examination and a practical guide enriched with case studies that bring to life the real-world applications and implications of AIED. The authors do not shy away from addressing the dual nature of AI's influence—its potential to enhance educational experiences and the accompanying risks that need vigilant management.

Through comprehensive chapters, they delve into critical issues such as inclusivity, efficacy, ethical considerations, and the safeguarding of student privacy. The narrative is both forward-thinking and grounded in the current realities faced by educational practitioners. This foreword aims to underscore the significance of this work for those of us tasked with steering educational institutions through an era of rapid technological change. "AI Changing the Arc of Educational Leadership" equips us with the knowledge and tools necessary to navigate this complex terrain, ensuring that AI serves as a force for good in our schools and communities.

Pinetop, AZ, USA   Mike Wright

CONTENTS

1 **Introduction** 1
What Are Wicked Problems? 5
References 6

2 **Understanding Artificial Intelligence in Education** 7
Students: Navigating Past Pandemics 9
Teachers: Bringing Back Autonomy 12
Educational Leaders: Engaging and Exploring AI Options 14
Parents and the Public: Alleviating Fears and Building Trust 16
Harms: Developing Leaders' Spidey Senses 20
Benefits: Supporting All Students 25
References 27

3 **Artificial Intelligence and Changing the Arc of Education** 33
Generation: Teaching Thoughtful Inquiry 34
Assessment: Finding Compatibility 39
Adaptation: Co-opting AI 43
Efficacy: Using to One's Capacity 45
Standards Managing Preparation 46
Policies: Building Up to Best Use 51
References 56

4 Ensuring Artificial Intelligence Changes the Arc of Education for Good   61

Emotions: Centering Students and Teachers   62

Explainability: Opening Black Boxes   67

Trust: Safeguarding Student Privacy and Watching the Watchers   74

Responsible Ethical Leaders   77

Ethical Strategies   83

Potential: Asking the Right Questions   86

References   87

5 Conclusion   91

References   93

Index   95

CHAPTER 1

Introduction

Abstract This chapter introduces artificial intelligence in education and sets up the framework for the book. The book includes a survey of approaches to AI in schools, considerations for inclusion, and considerations for limitations. These approaches are framed around the idea of wicked problems in education. With wicked problems, we cannot expect solutions to arise when the field is still young and in movement. However, by including the voices of educators and case studies in this book, we hope to encourage productive and meaningful conversations addressing these problems.

Keywords Artificial intelligence in education (AIED) • Wicked problems • Educational leaders • Ethical leadership

On a book on artificial intelligence (AI) in education, we should start with a definition of AI. We discuss a few more definitions in later sections of the book, but Murphy offered a clear definition: "applications of software algorithms and techniques that allow computers and machines to simulate human perception and decision- making processes to successfully complete tasks" (Murphy, 2019, p. 2). In other words, AI encompasses technology that can gather information and use that information to make decisions and complete tasks at a level similar to that of a human.

K. Moran Jackson, R. Papa, *AI Changing the Arc of Educational Leadership*, https://doi.org/10.1007/978-3-031-71415-3_1

Technology that acts like a human and takes over the world is a familiar trope in science fiction. Yet, with the growing public use of AI, we are starting to have a more realistic understanding of what AI is capable of at the moment. Most of what we discuss in this book falls under the *narrow AI* framework that views AI technology as confined to a limited structure in terms of its analysis and output. Generative AI applications, such as ChatGPT and Bard, which are as fantastical as their output may seem, are examples of narrow AI in that there are still limits to the types of data they can process, the types of analysis they can use, and the types of output they can produce.

Strong AI or artificial general intelligence (AGI) is not possible at this time, or at least not admitted to by AI researchers (Romero, 2023). Strong AI is the stuff of science fiction nightmares and futurists dreams where AI develops the ability to reason, make long-term strategic decisions across domains, and have the capacity to apply new behaviors or outputs across domains (Tegmark, 2017). Although the fear of strong AI can drive large parts of the conversation around future planning for AI in education, it has limited practicality to discuss at this point as no current applications exhibit these capabilities and current estimates place such skills far in the future (Zhang et al., 2022). Thus, we refrain from much speculation in this area.

Holmes et al. (2019; Holmes & Porayska-Pomsta, 2023) divided the subject of AI in education into four segments. First, *learning with AI* involves how AI can help students in the classroom, either through classroom applications or school administration systems. Second, *using AI to learn about learning* is a way that researchers and educators can use data mining and other AI-based tools to analyze educational data. Third, *learning about AI* is what you are doing by reading this book. It covers everything from teaching young children about data privacy to teaching graduate students the details of natural language processing. Finally, AI in education includes *preparing for AI* which is seen as the action steps people can take once they learn about AI.

We hope that you will feel confident to take preparatory steps for using AI in your life and in your schools after reading this book. To move you along that road, we offer a case study for consideration in each chapter. Before moving to the next section, read through the study and consider the questions at the end. We encourage you to have a conversation with another person about how you answered the questions.

The case studies highlight the often dueling and multiple concerns about how AI should be approached in educational spaces. We note clear, research supported advice for how to address some of these concerns. However, we also acknowledge that we are in a time of fast-moving change and paths forward are not always clear or may be context dependent. In other words, we are seeing the rise of wicked problems from AI in education.

Wicked problems are problems that are "complex, intractable, open-ended, unpredictable" (Alford & Head, 2017, p. 397). Educational leaders often deal with wicked problems but wicked problems caused by the growing abilities of AI are new. We have written this book to help preservice and inservice educators approach these new wicked problems with greater understanding and to consider how these problems fit within the educational landscape.

Jordan et al. suggest that to approach wicked problems, we "need wicked responses and wicked actions" (2014, p. 422). We cannot expect simple approaches or simple solutions to these types of problems. Rather, we need to carefully observe the context of the problem, being curious enough to gather more data from multiple viewpoints. We cannot simply expect, "to adopt a model that has worked elsewhere, whether a classroom across the hall, a school down the street, or a system in Finland" (p. 423). A panel of experts will also not suffice. We need multiple viewpoints at the table to share experiences, generate responses, and offer continual feedback on the system. Thus, the first chapter of this book addresses AI use in education from the viewpoints of various educational stakeholders. We write about how these groups view and approach AI in their educational work. The second chapter focuses on specific terminology, knowledge, and applications of AI use by educators who are currently in our schools. The third and last chapter expands on these classroom and district uses to consider the larger implications of AI use in school—what are the ethical and societal implications of such use. These are truly new wicked problems that we are currently encountering in our schools and will profoundly change the arc of our educational systems.

So how can we approach these wicked problems if they are just being encountered now? Alford and Head (2017) contribute to our discussion by offering a framework for viewing problems along two dimensions of difficulty. The first is how defined or knowable are the causes and solutions to the problem. Problems with known causes and obvious solutions are not wicked problems. We are within the realm of wickedness when people find it difficult to articulate a cause or an adequate solution to the problem. Second, Alfred and Head would have us note the degree of relatedness or agreeableness of the people involved in addressing the problem. People who are willing to discuss the problem and see others' viewpoints will minimize a wicked problem. If there are many stakeholders holding multiple viewpoints and not looking to compromise, we are again walking into wickedness.

We hope you will join us by approaching AI in education using a similar lens of agreeableness. We can start by thinking about the characteristics of the problem and about the stakeholders. This simple dichotomy offers a way to start addressing the issue. Alford and Head caution that "it is also important to understand that for decision-makers, this entails *making a judgement* on how to handle an issue, rather than pretending the decision can be 'read off' or derived from a *precise scientific estimate*" (2017, p. 409, italics in original). To build readers' skills to address wicked problems of AI in education, we present three case studies in the book. The case studies are loosely based on how educators and educational leaders might need to address AI concerns with other professionals, with students, and with parents and the public. The case studies are broken into three parts and are followed by questions for discussion. The questions are built to tap into how to approach wicked problems as discussed by Jordan et al. (2014) and Alford and Head (2017).

> If there is no "root cause" of "wickedness," there can be no single best approach to tackling such problems. If, for example, it is claimed that the fundamental cause of wicked problems is lack of scientific knowledge (e g about climate change), this claim already implies a solution—more scientific research to reduce uncertainty and to convince those who are sceptical of the mainstream science consensus. On the other hand, if the fundamental problem is seen to be divergence of viewpoints, the implied solution is to establish processes of inclusive participation that can lead towards a workable consensus. (Alford & Head, 2017, p. 410)

Similarly, there will be no single best approach to the use of AI in your schools. Different problems will call for different solutions. What we hope to share in this book are a variety of approaches to AI in schools, considerations for inclusion, and considerations for limitations. Wicked problems in education have been around for a long time and we cannot expect solutions to AI-related ones to arise with total agreement and understanding when the field is still so young. However, as emerging and practicing educators, we can have productive and meaningful conversations about how to address these problems that consider the viewpoints of others. We hope this book will aid you in having these conversations.

What Are Wicked Problems?

Wicked problems were initially defined by Rittel and Webber in 1973. They created a list of ten characteristics of wicked problems that are still referenced in the literature to this day.

1. There is no definitive formulation of a wicked problem.
2. Wicked problems have no "stopping rule" (i.e., no definitive solution).
3. Solutions to wicked problems are not true or false, but good or bad.
4. There is no immediate and no ultimate test of a solution to a wicked problem.
5. Every (attempted) solution to a wicked problem is a "one-shot operation"; the results cannot be readily undone, and there is no opportunity to learn by trial and error.
6. Wicked problems do not have an enumerable (or an exhaustively describable) set of potential solutions, nor is there a well-described set of permissible operations that may be incorporated into the plan.
7. Every wicked problem is essentially unique.
8. Every wicked problem can be considered to be a symptom of another problem.
9. The existence of a discrepancy representing a wicked problem can be explained in numerous ways.
10. The planner has no "right to be wrong" (i.e., there is no public tolerance of experiments that fail). (Head & Alford, 2015, p. 714)

Have you encountered wicked problems in your schools? In the literature you have read for class? How have you approached an understanding of these problems?

Which was more difficult to define: the cause of the problem or the solution to the problem? Or were both nebulous?

Were the stakeholders cooperative or contradictory? How did that help or hinder how people approached the problem?

Did a resolution to the problem ever arise? If yes, did observations, curiosity, or gathering multiple viewpoints help at any point in devising a resolution? If no, do you think a different resolution would have arisen with these steps?

REFERENCES

Alford, J., & Head, B. W. (2017). Wicked and less wicked problems: A typology and a contingency framework. *Policy and Society, 36*(3), 397–413. https://doi.org/10.1080/14494035.2017.1361634

Head, B. W., & Alford, J. (2015). Wicked problems: Implications for public policy and management. *Administration & Society, 47*(6), 711–739. https://doi.org/10.1177/0095399713481601

Holmes, W., & Porayska-Pomsta, K., Eds. (2023). *The ethics of artificial intelligence in education: Practices, challenges, and debates.* Routledge. https://doi.org/10.4324/9780429329067

Holmes, W., Bialik, M., & Fadel, C. (2019). *Artificial intelligence in education: Promises and implications for teaching and learning.* Center for Curriculum Redesign.

Jordan, M. E., Kleinsasser, R. C., & Roe, M. F. (2014). Wicked problems: Inescapable wickedity. *Journal of Education for Teaching, 40*(4), 415–430. https://doi.org/10.1080/02607476.2014.929381

Murphy, R. F. (2019). *Artificial intelligence applications to support K–12 teachers and teaching: A review of promising applications, challenges, and risks.* RAND Corporation. https://www.rand.org/pubs/perspectives/PE315.html

Romero, A. (2023, June 23). *AGI has been achieved internally.* The Algorithmic Bridge. https://www.thealgorithmicbridge.com/p/agi-has-been-achieved-internally

Tegmark, M. (2017). *Life 3.0: Being human in the age of artificial intelligence.* Knopf.

Zhang, B., Dreksler, N., Anderljung, M., Kahn, L., Giattino, C., Dafoe, A., & Horowitz, M. C. (2022). Forecasting AI progress: Evidence from a survey of machine learning researchers. *arXiv.* https://doi.org/10.48550/ARXIV.2206.04132

CHAPTER 2

Understanding Artificial Intelligence in Education

Abstract This chapter considers artificial intelligence (AI) in education, reviewing the scope and impact of current applications on students, teachers, educational leaders, parents, and the public. The chapter covers the major users of AI in education and how these groups of people interact with the applications in school settings. The chapter also covers the general benefits (increased motivation, personalization, timely feedback, and time savings) and harms (equal access, overdependence, perpetuating bias, privacy violations, fictitious data, and deepfakes) of using AI in schools.

Keywords Artificial intelligence in education (AIED) • Students • Teachers • Educational leaders • Parents

There are different definitions of AI. A technically focused definition comes from the Organization for Economic Cooperation and Development (2024):

> An AI system is a machine-based system that, for explicit or implicit objectives, infers, from the input it receives, how to generate outputs such as predictions, content, recommendations, or decisions that can influence physical or virtual environments. Different AI systems vary in their levels of autonomy and adaptiveness after deployment. (p. 7)

© The Author(s), under exclusive license to Springer Nature
Switzerland AG 2024
K. Moran Jackson, R. Papa, *AI Changing the Arc of Educational
Leadership*, https://doi.org/10.1007/978-3-031-71415-3_2

Another definition of AI that places it within the context of human environments comes from UNICEF (2021):

> AI refers to machine-based systems that can, given a set of human-defined objectives, make predictions, recommendations, or decisions that influence real or virtual environments. AI systems interact with us and act on our environment, either directly or indirectly. Often, they appear to operate autonomously, and can adapt their behaviour by learning about the context. (p. 13)

And yet another definition, this time from Holmes et al. (2023), built on work by Eynon and Young (2021), states that "AI is a complex socio-technical artefact that needs to be understood as something that is constructed through complex social processes" (p. 18). This last definition of AI recognizes the social construction of AI, the importance of how we define *intelligence*, and how we construct a system to enact that kind of intelligence.

The definitions of intelligence have changed over time and have become more complex. As educators, we are often reminded that intelligence cannot be well-defined and can take multiple forms, most exemplified by the popularity of Gardner's theory of multiple intelligences. "According to Gardner, an intelligence involves a person's ability to solve a problem or do something considered valuable in one or more cultures" (Morgan, 2021, p. 126). With this broad view of intelligence, consider how even one-hundred years ago, the most common smartphone, with its abilities to remind us of project deadlines and read text aloud, might well have been considered intelligent.

These overlapping definitions of artificial intelligence with a broad view of intelligence feed into the current common educational experiences of using intelligent technology in our schools and classrooms. If we can define an intelligent agent or application as something that "solves a problem" or "makes a prediction," then our classrooms have been riddled with AI for a long time. The current distinction brought by specialized AI applications is the broad sweep and impact of the applications beyond specialized tasks. The change these tools are bringing to the educational arc is being experienced differently by different stakeholders. We want to start our tour of the impact of AI in education with students.

STUDENTS: NAVIGATING PAST PANDEMICS

The coronavirus disease (COVID-19) pandemic that stretched across the 2020–2022 school years brought educational technology (ed-tech) to the forefront of public debates about education. Prior to the pandemic, ed-tech had become an increasingly important aspect of education, but with the pandemic, the use of programs and applications moved from within the school setting into living rooms and kitchen tables. This expanded presence came with a large price tag for schools. For illustration, in 2021 at the height of the pandemic, spending on global ed-tech venture funding was at an all-time high of $20.8 billion, an order of magnitude greater than the $2.97 billion subsequently spent in 2023 (Riddell, 2024). Large funding influxes poured into schools from local and national governments to buy equipment that would allow students to stay connected to their teachers and peers while isolated at home. As more technology was implemented during the pandemic, the ed-tech experience of students moved from viewing a projection of a teacher's computer at the front of a classroom, to viewing a Chromebook screen in front of their face every school moment.

While the public became concerned about the growing use of ed-tech and children's resultant overexposure to screens, how artificial intelligence was often a hidden partner in pandemic ed-tech applications was less recognized. The eye tracking software that was measuring how often students looked away from a screen when taking an online exam was driven by AI vision software. The math application that determined if a student was ready for a unit quiz was using machine learning algorithms for that determination. Sometimes without much knowledge of those involved, AI was making decisions and influencing the education of students. For example, AI applications were largely responsible for eye tracking as part of testing technology that then alerted educators to possible cheating, a potentially life-altering insinuation.

AI applications operate in three different ways as educational tools, according to Ouyang and Jiao (2021). AI can be the leader of the learning process, choosing materials, content, and testing. AI could also be collaborative, working with the student through the learning process, and weighing student input with other predetermined goals. Finally, AI can be empowering, leaving the student to take charge of the learning process, using AI as a tool under their control. Ouyand and Jiao termed these paradigms AI-directed, AI-supported, and AI-empowered.

Many of the people who argue that AI is the next natural step in ed-tech and general education often envision AI-directed learning tools. In this view, AI systems largely replace or assist teachers in creating personalized learning experiences for each student. The AI system allows for the personalization of content already aligned and verified as relevant to the standards. Students largely learn the same content, but the content will be made relevant to student interests and to their learning needs. Is one student interested in sports and another interested in astronomy? Then for a reading unit, the first student will read about sports heroes and the second will read about astronauts. For a math unit, these students will solve math problems by calculating batting averages or rocket speeds. Both can learn the same content but geared toward their special interests. While this personalization may speak to the interests of learners, educators need to consider how individual modifications may also narrow the definition of a general education.

For AI-empowered learning many educators turn to collaborative learning and project-based learning. Ng et al. (2022) described a few collaborative learning projects that had students work with both each other and with AI, either through role playing or designing an AI model. These types of projects match with the need to educate students beyond content, to 21st century skills such as critical thinking, creativity, and collaboration. The move to more collaborative work using AI matches with a trend toward more collaborative work in general that happened during and after the pandemic. As discussed by a large urban public school central office administrator:

> [During the pandemic, we were] in the K 12 setting where there's just no way our kids can be online for a full day. And then the way we're teaching also has to shift. It has to adjust. ... We're shifting away from a lot of that lecture or teacher led [classes]. We were saying, do more of the collaborative or group work. Let your students do some of that work and explore their learning. You provide some of the resources for them to explore. But it was a very large shift for our teachers. (Nava, 2023)

That so many students are already using AI in their homes and in their schools, even if they may not know it, has led many in the public to argue that we need to be directly teaching students about AI (Forbes, n.d.). In other words, AI needs to be not only a tool for learning, but also a subject of the curriculum. Several proposals have been made about what students need to learn about AI. Touretzky et al. (2019) suggested that potential student AI content knowledge be divided into five *big ideas*: (1) perception, (2) representation and reasoning, (3) learning, (4) natural interaction, and (5) societal impact. Under this framework, the curriculum for students on AI should include how AI systems take in information using sensors; how AI systems represent that information in their data storage and how they operate on that information; how AI systems can generate new knowledge by analysis of the information; how AI systems can interact with humans to gather or share information; and how all of these actions can have an impact on human society. Categories of knowledge, such as being able to define natural language processing or describe the use of training data, would fall under one or more of these various big ideas.

While academics might argue about the ideal components of an AI curricula, school systems across the globe are in the process of writing these curricula. Ng et al. (2022) recounted the following curriculum development projects underway:

- The Education Ministry in China developed an AI textbook for use in K-12 in 2018.
- In Europe, a project called AI+ is developing high school AI curricula.
- In Taiwan, the Ministry of Education is requiring AI educational materials to be used in primary and secondary schools.

So how do students feel about the growing use of AI in their schools? Some research points to how students are approaching AI with both excitement and worry. A survey by the Walton Family Foundation in 2023 found that "most students think [ChatGPT] can help them become better students (68%) and help them learn faster (75%)" (Impact Research, 2023, p. 1). A Pew Research Center survey found that of the two-thirds of US teenagers who had heard of ChatGPT, 69 percent believe it can ethically be used to research topics, but much lower percentages of teens endorsed using it to solve math problems (39 percent) or write essays (20 percent; Sidoti & Gottfried, 2023). In a survey in the US, England, and Wales, secondary students reported that they were worried about the impact of AI on their job prospects, and that they will not be able "to reach their full potential in a generative AI world" (MathWorks, 2024, para. 5). The students in the survey also endorsed the need to learn about AI ethics as part of classroom curriculum.

TEACHERS: BRINGING BACK AUTONOMY

If AI is touted for students as a tool for engagement and personalization, then for teachers AI is envisioned as a way to enact best practices. With AI, educators could in theory identify and address students' specific educational shortfalls, personalize content to the interests of multiple students, and allow students to move at their pace rather than at the pace of the larger group. These goals have been put on educators in the past but have found it difficult to implement under practicalities of the current educational structure.

Recent surveys of teachers about their perceptions and attitudes toward AI are building a generally positive, but cautious, perspective. One survey of US public school teachers found that while two-thirds of them did not use AI applications, three-quarters of the teachers expected to use AI in the future (Diliberti et al., 2024). Both non-AI users and AI-users reported their barriers to future use of AI included "concerns about the role of AI in society as a whole," "concerns about data privacy," and lack of professional development and guidelines around AI use (Diliberti et al., 2024, p. 9). Another US national survey of teachers and students by the Walton Family Foundation in 2023 found that more than three-quarters of teachers felt that ChatGPT could "help them grow as teachers" and of those who used the program 88% felt that "it's had a positive impact" (Impact Research, 2023, pp. 1–2). US public school teachers in a Pew Research Center survey expressed mixed feelings about AI (Lin, 2024). While only 6 percent of participants thought AI offers more benefits than harms, a quarter felt the opposite and the remainder were either not sure or believed the benefits and harms were balanced. There were differences by grade level in perceptions, with 35 percent of high school teachers endorsing the harmful stance while 47 percent of elementary teachers were unsure.

A large urban public school Central Office Administrator noted that teachers have had varying exposure to AI applications:

> We're just starting to learn about this AI. I mean, the most popular is the chat GPT. I think that's, that's very popular. And we're all starting to kind of explore that and see what the ramifications mean for us in our work. But it's still very new to us. I think, at the at the district level in terms of that, that usage, it's probably a very small number of people who are using it or are more familiar with it. And those would be some of our computer science teachers or science teachers or our steam or stem instructors. And I think there's from the other disciplines, like humanities, and I think they may be a little more reticent to embrace or even engage in that. (Nava, 2023)

One of the most common ways to categorize teacher approaches to technology in general is through the Technology, Pedagogy, and Content Knowledge (TPACK) model (Mishra & Koehler, 2006; Kabakci Yurdakul et al., 2012). TPACK allows us to separate teachers' understandings of different technologies and their application in classrooms. Using a three-pronged model, teachers' first component of understanding is the content knowledge they have about the subject they are teaching. The second component is knowledge about technology. In the case of AI, this aspect could include specific knowledge, such as the ability to define algorithmic biases or the ability to provide a high-level overview of machine learning. Finally, teachers have pedagogical knowledge such as how to effectively use exit questions or how to evaluate student projects. The combination of these three areas plays a role in how teachers approach and use technology within their classrooms. In the case of AI, someone with high technological and pedagogical understanding might include techniques such as incorporating AI applications in project-based learning or creating differentiated readings from an AI application. Teachers might well have made these same pedagogical and content choices without including technology—creating readings or a project—but the choice to include or not include AI technology will result from the interplay of the three TPACK components.

How teachers approach AI applications has some association with teacher content knowledge. A public urban university technologist noted the difference for classes that require students to learn specific content knowledge versus skill sets:

> *The sciences are really unique ... Not all in science have this care, obviously, but within the science that is known, when somebody is using Chat GPT, it is not relevant. It's not important because the science would have been known anyway. In other words, if you're about to teach cell biology, and a student gets ahead of you by writing a paper on it via Chat GPT, all he did is simply get ahead of the information. ... But of course, you had the assessments you used to have to do. You have the in-class midterms, in-class finals that you still have to do. So you can always gauge the learning based on that. But I think I think that the harder part will be for the arts, the liberal arts, in the language arts, all the disciplines that require and expect ... original thought. The problem is that most things have already been written, like 80% has already been written. ... Most of what students write nowadays, it's a variation what's already been written. (Martinez, 2023)*

Case study #1:
Part A
Following a survey taken during the start of year inservice, the professional development director at a large suburban school district found that the elementary school teachers in his district wanted to know more about how to use AI in their teaching. The director decided that since he did not know much about AI and with the school year already underway, they would pay for an AI expert from a local college to give a presentation to one school during a planned inservice session and be live-streamed to other schools that wanted to participate. The session could also be recorded and then played during meetings later in the year at other schools. For these schools, the teacher tech-leaders would head a discussion about AI with their fellow teachers.

What topics would you consider essential for the expert to cover in their introduction to AI?

What NPBEA (2015) standards, if any, should be the focal points of the program (see https://www.npbea.org/psel/ for the standards)? Why are these standards relevant to the topic? What needs surrounding AI professional development might not be addressed in the standards?

EDUCATIONAL LEADERS: ENGAGING AND EXPLORING AI OPTIONS

One of the most common calls surrounding AI and education has been the call for rules and policies regarding AI use in schools. Administrators and other educational leaders in schools and districts have been forced to act or not and to justify or not these actions. Many schools have formed advisory committees made of teachers and administrators to address these concerns, leading to different responses across the US. In attempts to standardize responses, leaders of the states' departments of education have started issuing guidelines about use. Within the first two weeks of 2024 alone, four different states released their AI guidelines. (See Chap. 2 for further discussion.)

As the national standards for educational leaders issued by the National Policy Board for Educational Administration (NPBEA) were issued in 2015, they contain no reference to AI. However, standards 4(e) and 9(f) state that effective leaders "promote the effective use of technology in the service of teaching and learning" and "employ technology to improve the quality and efficiency of operations and management" (pp. 10, 23). Many would argue that the advantages offered by AI would be beneficial to both of these categories and that effective leaders would employ, if not promote, AI use.

However, there are other standards and considerations for educational leaders to consider when deploying AI in their schools. These other concerns may reason against students' and teachers' access to AI tools in the classroom. For example, standard 7(b) asks leaders to "empower and entrust teachers and staff with collective responsibility for meeting the academic, social, emotional, and physical needs of each student, pursuant to the mission, vision, and core values of the school." The use of AI software that reads and monitors employer emails may be seen as antithetical to the vision of empowerment and trust, taking away from collective responsibility.

Educational leaders have conflicting roles when it comes to using AI systems in their schools. They have a responsibility to make sure that teachers and consequently, students, are prepared to act on twenty-first century knowledge. Putting a limit or outright prohibition on all AI use in schools would not uphold this requirement. Leaders also have to allow teachers some autonomy to experiment with technologies that have the potential to enhance their teaching practice and student outcomes. These goals would put leaders on the front lines of encouraging AI within schools. A public university professor of technology discussed this dichotomy:

> *It's not about the technology. It's about how we think about technology, and how it can support learning and growth within our classrooms. … How do we use that technology? Or how do we need to prepare people to think about those technologies? Not just in that critical sense as, why am I using it? When am I using it? Who's going to use it? How do we make sure that it's going to be used in a way that is not harmful to anyone and that predicts growth? … We can grow from that. Let's have a conversation about that … Making sure that we're growing with our students and … we really have to be open to continual change.* (Armfield, 2023)

Leaders also have to be concerned with aspects of AI that put their teachers and students at risk, such as the loss of privacy or untested technology. They also have the fiscal responsibility to maintain good governance around school funds being used for products or services that are tested and have a track record of school improvement. These concerns would discourage the use of AI in our schools without additional safeguards or a history of effective use.

There have been some attempts at a large scale to provide information to educators and the public about the capacity and efficacy of commercial AI products used in schools. Williamson (2021) described some meta-edtech organizations that are designed "to educate leaders, teachers and procurement specialists about the evidence for 'what works' in educational technology" (p. 2). The Evidence Exchange (https://edtechevidence.org/) in the US and EdTech Impact (https://edtechimpact.com/) in the United Kingdom both offer reviews and information on various applications and software that target schools. However, the goal of these sites could be argued to mainly be commercial, with perhaps limited views of what constitutes "evidence" and less opening to "alternative social, political and cultural explanations to the impact and market-led approaches" (Williamson, 2021, p. 5).

Parents and the Public: Alleviating Fears and Building Trust

Parents are divided, as is the public, in how they want schools to approach AI. Some parents are hungry for their children to learn about the newest technology, seeing such education as preparing their students for the future and enabling them to obtain tech-focused jobs that have traditionally been sites of economic and social security and advancement. Other parents worry about an excess focus on technology would be detrimental to other critical skills. A rural public school superintendent described the mix of parental attitudes they see in their district:

> *You got that group that no matter what you're doing is wrong. And then you have another group that are, because of their situation, they're disengaged. They're just trying to survive. The parents that I'd say are have been always involved and will continue to be involved, have the normal concerns about screen time. And are we trying to replace the interaction with teachers and direct instruction with the program? And if we are, what does that program look like? And was it teaching my kid? How effective is it? All of those concerns, the wide spectrum of parental concerns, I think you see everywhere, almost on every issue.* (Wright, 2023)

Previous research has shown that when parents control technologies such as social media, this supervision helps with generating positive child outcomes (Fardouly et al., 2018). Parents may worry that a lack of similar control over access to AI in schools will not allow their children to develop the interpersonal and intrapersonal skills that are needed for many more jobs. This worry has even driven some parents to insist on tech-free schools for their children, especially for the youngest. However, unless educators are working at such a school with a self-selected parent population, they will have parents of all views in their schools and will need to navigate calls for both more and less AI use.

While research on parental attitudes toward artificial intelligence in education is limited at this time, generally parents have positive attitudes toward the use of ICT in classrooms, although not to the same extent as teachers (Ramírez-Rueda et al., 2021). This study of parents and teachers in preschool and primary schools in Spain also found that parents of primary aged children had more favorable attitudes toward ICT use in schools than did parents of preschool students.

Besides offering opinions on how AI is used by their children in schools, parents may also be consumers of AI ed-tech products. In 2016, when AI systems were starting to gain use in education, Luckin et al. (2016) hypothesized that AI systems could provide support to low-income parents from low-resourced communities. Because the systems had access to vast stores of knowledge, the use of AI would possibly allow these parents to provide more academic readiness skills for their children. The authors optimistically argued that "AIEd assistants should be available for all parents, with additional support provided to those parents who need it most" and that parents should be included in AI application design processes (Luckin et al., 2016, p. 43).

However, this possibility has not appeared in a material way. Many AI systems are generated by for-profit organizations and there is a noticeable positive relationship between AI users and income, such that people with more economic and social resources were more likely to access common AI applications than others without these resources (Pahl, 2023). The concern with such inequality is that parents who are already placed ahead in resources will be able to use AI to keep their children ahead. Without equal access, and some would argue affirmative access, parents and children with less resources will likely only continue to face barriers. For example, when writing college admissions essays, access to advanced grammar and editing AI services would place those who use these services at an advantage to those who do not. Access to these AI applications could amplify inequalities already present in educational systems. Educators need to be well-versed on the potentials and outcomes of such divisions.

Parents also report their own troubling behaviors with technology that could impact how they interact with their children. In one study, three-quarters of parents with children under the age of 5 reported that smart-phones interfered with their time with their children and close to two-thirds reported that they had trouble controlling the impulse to check their messages (Glassman et al., 2021). This same study also revealed that parents who were aware of their problematic technology use were open to the use of AI applications that could help alert them to their misuse around their children.

Just as educators and educational leaders struggle with wicked problems of AI integration in schools, parents are struggling with AI integration in their home lives.

> This overwhelming influence of digital technology on parenting has been largely attributed to the demanding rhythm of family life and a parent's need to tackle everyday obstacles. More and more parents encounter stressful situations due to great expectations issued by the marketing industry about "good parenting." More specifically, parents get convinced that a surveillance routine is necessary for being a responsible and careful parent through the use of various mobile apps and digital devices in addition to using social media and various websites to train themselves in responsible parenting. However, digital parenting tools tend to focus on the protective and preventive features [Zaman & Nouwen, 2016] while almost entirely discarding the issues related to the ethical approach of children's privacy. (Drigas et al., 2023, p. 123)

Parents are facing similar challenges to schools regarding wicked problems of child privacy versus child monitoring, of defining "good" in regards to both parenting and teaching, and of managing stress. However, educators are only now beginning to engage in dialogues with parents around these questions. As recounted by a large urban public school central office administrator:

> *With parents, I think there are conversations going on at the district level. We do have an entire department of families and communities, and they do a lot of work, a lot of engagement with parents. I think the conversations are just beginning around this. … I think right now it's just this idea that people are trying to get their mind around is very new to us. (Nava, 2023)*

Research by Kong (2018) found that similar to teachers, parents have a general positive regard for the use of technology in the form of e-learning and that they support technology use and activities in their homes. Notably, these parents also were interested in establishing technology policies at home that would align with policies used at school, such as screen-time limitations. This finding of the need for correspondence between schools and parents concerning child technology use was supported by research by Tsuei and Hsu (2019) who found that parents who experienced better parent–teacher communication had more positive attitudes toward the use of technology in their child's classroom. They also found that in general parents' positive attitudes toward technology use were correlated with their perceptions of the importance of technology.

Thus, as AI applications grow in public use and importance, there will likely be more calls for their use and integration in schools. The findings from these studies suggested to the authors (Kong, 2018; Tsuei & Hsu, 2019) that schools can and should take a proactive role in establishing technology literacy programs for parents. These programs can include workshops and prescribed parent–child activities. As recent discussions about school technology increasingly address AI, the need for schools to reach out to parents also increases.

The public may also put additional demands on educators through public pressure. As school board meetings become increasingly popular places to voice social expectations and desires, we may see more members of the public addressing these concerns in meetings. We may also see pressure through media reports and social media, even from people not directly connected with our schools.

Luckin et al. in 2016 posited that over time, our public systems will develop AI infrastructure systems, similar to our electrical and road systems. If so, at that point, educational systems will have to find ways to standardize their systems. Luckin et al. state:

> True progress will require the development of an AIEd infrastructure. This will not, however, be a single monolithic AIEd system. Instead, it will resemble the marketplace that has developed for smartphone apps: hundreds and then thousands of individual AIEd components, developed in collaboration with educators, conformed to uniform international data standards, and shared with researchers and developers worldwide. These standards will enable system-level data collation and analysis that help us learn much more about learning itself and how to improve it." (2016, p. 12)

In developing such standards, the public and policymakers will undoubtedly have a say in what happens within the educational AI system. However, how much say is still debatable. We will discuss the implications of policy making on AI use in schools in a subsequent chapter.

Case Study #1
Part B
The director received feedback from the teachers and administrators at the schools that the AI training being provided was unsatisfactory. Most of the comments said that the training was too high-level and concerned with policies around AI, rather than the practical concerns about how a teacher would use a specific program in a classroom. They also felt that the training was geared more toward teachers with older students. A few teachers also mentioned that the presenter did not mention how AI could be used with students with disabilities. The director decided to ask teachers who had participated in the training to provide more detailed feedback with the intention of creating a new program for the next school year.

Imagine that you are a tech-savvy teacher who is excited about using AI in the classroom. What kind of training would you like to see?

Imagine that you are a new teacher, nervous about using AI in the classroom. What kind of training would be beneficial for you?

Can the director design a program that addresses the different needs of different teachers? How should training for teachers differ from training for administrators surrounding AI use in education?

Harms: Developing Leaders' Spidey Senses

As mentioned in earlier sections, AI applications in education are not without the potential for harm. We have already touched on several factors, including equal access and overdependence. While generative AI applications have some unique risks, all AI applications share some risks of perpetuating societal inequalities. This risk arises from the development of AI applications based on biased data (Benjamin, 2019). Data can perpetuate societal bias, either by being collected in biased formats or losing important contextual, qualitative information in the codification process.

The rural public school superintendent addressed student data and the district's approach.

> *With any software program or any use of technology, we're always worried about the safeguarding student data, and student information and privacy, frankly, and so there's been a lot of effort invested for a small district ... Student data belongs to us. The safeguards are an IT question that's way out of my wheelhouse, but we formed what we called a tiger team, and it had an administrator, parents, a school board member, and the technology team. These are people that for a relatively small district have the capacity of a much larger district within our IT. They looked at security data, making sure that we're not sharing data improperly or accessible by anyone else, but certain teachers. And so, I know that there are login credentials required. We do a whole another set of security measures before you can even get into these tools. You have to go through our own internal set up to make sure that we're screening people that are trying to come in and get this data. The data belongs to us, it belongs to the parent and the student, and it's our job to safeguard it. So, we're not sharing with anybody else.* (Wright, 2023)

The inherent nature of AI bias is readily apparent as it does not have human "lived experiences" along a spectrum of differences and frailties among culture, gender, age, special needs, race, etc. A technologist at a public urban university described how these potential risks can generate fear in educators:

> *In many ways, I think this is magnifying little biases we had before. ... Faculty, they all have biases, but this thing [AI] has really magnified it because it's made people less aware of what the potential is. ... Because they don't know the possibilities, they're more afraid of it, and therefore magnifying their own insecurity and bias, in terms of what their students can and should be able to accomplish with tools like this. And I think some faculty are doing good. I think some faculty are doing excellent in how they manage it. ... But a lot more than not, are not doing so well.* (Martinez, 2023)

One of the most important references for evaluating the potential harm in US schools is the federal government's Family Educational Rights and Privacy Act (FERPA), which limits what kind of information about students can be collected and shared. AI tools, which often collect and store information gathered from interactions with people, can be at risk of violating FERPA (ILO Group, 2024; Westrope, 2023). As further explained by guidance from the Office of Educational Technology of the US Department of Education:

> What happens to this data, how it is deleted, and who sees it is of huge concern to educators. As educators contemplate using AI-enabled technologies to assist in tackling educational inequities, they must consider whether the information about students shared with or stored in an AI-enabled system is subject to federal or state privacy laws, such as FERPA. Further, educators must consider whether interactions between students and AI systems create records that must be protected by law, such as when a chatbot or automated tutor generates conversational or written guidance to a student. Decisions made by AI technologies, along with explanations of those decisions that are generated by algorithms may also be records that must be protected by law. (2023, p. 33)

While we introduced some major aspects of current AI applications, we will talk more about some of the underlying engineering techniques underlying them in the following chapter. A basic understanding of applications and techniques is helpful for determining how to ensure safer implementation in schools. However, understanding the definitions and categorizing types of products can only get an educational leader so far. There is a need for leaders to develop their "spidey senses" which is a reference to the intuition and understanding of the staff and school context that makes effective implementation of programs possible (Cartwright, 2004; Dyer & Carothers, 2000; Hart, 2018). Educators need to be concerned not only with what a tool can do, but also with how it is being used.

> The ethical concerns, then, are not focused on AI but on the way in which AI is used and the consequences this use has. … This is not to suggest that AI is an ethically neutral tool, but rather to highlight that the broader context of AI use, which includes existing moral preferences, social practices and formal regulation, cannot be ignored when undertaking ethical reflection and analysis. (Stahl et al., 2023, p. 108)

Our book is guided by this concern with the ethical application of AI in schools. The arc of education has sometimes veered from centering the experiences of students; at these times, education has instead focused on the goals of the economic system (Kliebard, 2004). We believe education should be student centered. Thus, any discussions of how AI is implemented in schools should center student needs as a moral imperative.

A common concern with current AI applications is that they perpetuate stereotypes and inaccurate data on groups. One investigative analysis of images generated by AI applications showed pervasive stereotypes (Turk, 2023). For example, in 100 images of "a Mexican person," 99 included a sombrero, indicative of both stereotypes and lack of modern sensitivities, placing non-Western peoples as outside contemporary modes (para. 20). Other images were not only stereotypical, but also inaccurate. For example, when asked to produce images of "a plate of Chinese food," a significant number included an odd number of chopsticks which is unlucky in Chinese culture (para. 42–44). Other studies have documented similar biases, even when the AI is pretrained or data are curated before use. Such stereotypes present in AI applications risk not only perpetuating stereotypes, but also erasing diversity in our world, limiting creative applications and alternate worldviews (Benjamin, 2019; Garcia, 2016; Turk, 2023).

In the end, AI, like previous technologies incorporated into educational spaces, is a mediator of learning, not the focus of learning (Bower, 2019). What this means in practice is that AI allows people to more easily access knowledge, either within existing media or within networks of people. Researchers, such as Bower, note that when technology serves as a mediator, it is ultimately humans with "intentional agency" who are in control of the application, either through directing or programming the technology (2019, p. 1037). While this line might appear blurred in AI applications that are operating using an algorithm that has little human oversight, we must remember that the appearance of no human oversight is a planned design feature. Thus, risks of harm are not nebulous and unavoidable features of AI applications, but rather result from human decisions and, sometimes, misjudgments. As AI agents become more advanced, however, the weight of intentional agency may shift. Bower notes:

> On the one hand, a human or humans have at some point programmed the system to provide intelligent feedback and make intelligent pedagogical decisions, so in fact, the technology is still executing the will of humans, albeit in a less deterministic fashion. On the other hand, as artificial intelligence technologies become more autonomous, and the relationship between the underlying intentions of the human programmer and the actions of technology becomes less direct, it may be argued that technology is no longer a mediator but exercises independent intentional acts. (Bower, 2019, p. 1044)

AI applications known as large language models (LLMs) have been around a while now, long before ChatGPT-3 was released in 2020 to universal amazement (Lesiv, 2023). The mathematics underlying computer processing of written language had been worked out by the 1980s, but computers with the power to develop and apply the models beyond academic interest were still a few decades away. Additionally, the LLMs need to be trained on data and the amount of data needed was not available until the explosive growth of the Internet and the ability to capture billions of bits of language data created by millions of people. In 2018, ELMo[1], one of the first natural language processing models, worked with 94 million parameters. By June 2020, ChatGPT-3 had a neural network of more than 96 layers and 175 billion parameters. The extra data and power allowed ChatGPT-3 to perform sophisticated operations such as passing an MBA exam and writing advanced software code (Lesiv, 2023). Later models, such as ChatGPT-4, are reported to have more than 100 layers and 100 trillion parameters (Fenjiro, 2023). Most of these later applications are built on multimodal models, versus large language models. Multimodal models can use text and images as input and produce text and images as output, whereas LLMs are usually restricted to a single transformation based on their programming, such as text to text or image to text.

Both LLMs and multimodal AI applications depend on a neural network architecture using a transformer model. Neural networks can leverage several layers of input, incorporating large amounts of data points, such as days of attendance or time to answer a test item. These input categories, or *parameters*, are weighted for their ability to contribute to a solution. This weighing process takes place over several layers, with the goal of producing the most accurate solution, as decided by the programmers. Transformer models permit several bits of information to be connected to each other and processed simultaneously. This advancement allows the model to maintain information from different parts of a prompt, rather than proceeding sequentially, leading to more multifaceted answers. In a broad sense, the technical advancements in neural network architecture and transformer models allowed for applications to take a more

---

[1] Fun fact. Many AI models developed after ELMo (Embeddings from Language Models) are also named after characters on Sesame Street, as a nod to this original model. This include BERT (Bidirectional Encoder Representations from Transformers), ERNIE (Enhanced Representation through Knowledge Integration), KERMIT (Kontextuell Encoder Representations Made by Insertion Transformations), and Big BIRD (Big Bidirectional Insertion Representations for Documents). See Vincent (2019).

holistic approach to prompts posed by people. Rather than working through prescribed coding lists of if-then statements, these AI models are able to gather several inputs at once, such as a long text string or a complex visual image, and process them together to generate a novel answer.

The potential for harm with these advanced AI applications remains unknown because we have yet to see them used on a global scale. But some testing indicates where potential problems may lie based on the explosive growth in the use of LLM models. One potential issue with large language models is stochastic parroting. This phrase refers to the ability of AI applications to mimic human language, but without true understanding (Bender et al., 2021). Relatedly, another risk, especially with LLMs, is hallucinations, where the applications make up fake information, such as academic references or quotes (O'Brien, 2023). Especially for students these are real risks if they assume that these LLM and multimodal applications act similarly to web search applications. Web search applications will return real results, sometimes of dubious academic value, but sources that exist in some form and can be referenced. LLMs can easily create a reference to articles never written by known researchers, creating an imaginary journal title based on similar sounding published works. The applications, without additional programming, do not distinguish between the creation of a summary of research and the creation of a plausible reference for that research.

Another risk with generative AI applications of concern for educators is the risk of deepfakes. Deepfakes capture a person's voice or image and create a fake audio or video recording of that person. At the time of writing, there are no federal or state laws against deepfakes, although some are being proposed (Ruiz, 2024). Some schools can address deepfakes as violations of student codes of conduct, but the application of such codes has been inconsistent, similar to school approaches to cyberbullying (Ruiz, 2024). Many advocates are arguing that AI companies need to implement more safeguards to prevent and allow policing of deepfakes, but until that time, schools will find that they deal with the fallout for their students and teachers, as yet another wicked problem.

BENEFITS: SUPPORTING ALL STUDENTS

We do not want to end this chapter by scaring the reader about all the risks of AI. Rather, we want to end with more positive views of the potential benefits that can arise from integrating AI in our schools. Balancing potential risks and potential benefits shapes decision making for many educators and educational leaders. A public university professor of technology described the needed balance this way:

> *I think we have got to find some balance. When I'm talking about using AI, it's about balance, right? How do we use it to benefit us in the most potential way? But let's not forget, there needs to be human aspects of this right. ... We have got to find that balance what's best for our kids, what's best for our communities and go from there.* (Armfield, 2023)

Adiguzel et al. (2023) listed four notable benefits of using AI for students. First, AI applications have made a case that they can increase student motivation and interest in materials. This may be due to novelty, personalization, or autonomy. More research needs to be done to tease apart the causal effects. Second, AI applications can be personalized and provide rapid feedback. As discussed previously, academic work can also be personalized to student interest topics or academic levels. Additionally, rather than waiting a week for a paper to be returned, AI applications can evaluate and offer advice about areas for improvement. Although current evaluations are limited to rote and technical learning, researchers are working to improve the evaluative capabilities for written content and more complex products. Third, AI applications aid collaborative learning and communication, with the impacts most notably for language learners and students with disabilities. AI can be a tireless and supportive tutor for students who require immediate feedback on pronunciation or reading of words. Finally, Adiguzel et al. noted there is some research support that AI applications may help students deal with socio-emotional difficulties, such as low confidence, anxiety, and embarrassment. These students may feel more comfortable expressing themselves to what they believe to be a neutral computer than a real person, although educators should be aware of potential biases in AI applications.

Adiguzel et al. (2023) also argued that AI provides many benefits to teachers and administrators. First, by providing more information on student performance and alternative teaching methods, some AI programs may increase teachers' skills and development. Applications can help with the documenting and assessment chores performed by teachers, such as homework tracking and assignment grading. Additional AI applications can help with the more creative aspects of teaching, such as lesson planning or designing lectures. AI can also provide feedback that is useful for administrators by making predictions about potential outcomes, such as school enrollment patterns, cafeteria management, or monitoring student risk factors.

Case Study #1
Part C
The director is asked to speak about the program and training teachers to use AI at a board meeting. After the meeting, the director is surprised to be approached by parents who want to know more about the kind of AI being used by their children and how teachers are being trained to protect their children from data theft. Talking with the director of parent engagement, you both start discussing whether a workshop for parents on AI is needed.

How would you engage with parents about the need for a parent meeting on AI use in schools?

What could be some potential difficulties with opening up the topic to the broad parenting group versus creating a committee or leaving the topic to the schools? What are some of the potential benefits of engaging with a wider variety of parents at the district level?

References

Adiguzel, T., Kaya, M. H., & Cansu, F. K. (2023). Revolutionizing education with AI: Exploring the transformative potential of ChatGPT. *Contemporary Educational Technology*, *15*(3), ep429. https://doi.org/10.30935/cedtech/13152

Armfield, S. (2023). *Personal communication.*

Bender, E. M., Gebru, T., McMillan-Major, A., & Shmitchell, S. (2021). On the dangers of stochastic parrots: Can language models be too big?. *Proceedings of the 2021 ACM Conference on Fairness, Accountability, and Transparency,* 610–623. https://doi.org/10.1145/3442188.3445922

Benjamin, R. (2019). *Race after technology: Abolitionist tools for the New Jim Code.* Wiley. https://www.wiley.com/en-us/Race+After+Technology%3A+Abolitionist+Tools+for+the+New+Jim+Code-p-9781509526437

Bower, M. (2019). Technology-mediated learning theory. *British Journal of Educational Technology*, *50*(3), 1035–1048. https://doi.org/10.1111/bjet.12771

Cartwright, T. (2004). Feeling your way: Enhancing leadership through intuition. *Leadership in Action, 24*(2), 8–11. https://doi.org/10.1002/lia.1060

Diliberti, M., Schwartz, H. L., Doan, S., Shapiro, A. K., Rainey, L., & Lake, R. J. (2024). *Using artificial intelligence tools in K-12 classrooms.* RAND. https://www.rand.org/content/dam/rand/pubs/research_reports/RRA900/RRA956-21/RAND_RRA956-21.pdf

Drigas, A., Karyotaki, M., & Skianis, C. (2023). Mobiles, digital tech, empathy, metacognition, self-consciousness and the role of parents in schools and societies of the future. *International Journal of Interactive Mobile Technologies (iJIM), 17*(07), 118–132. https://doi.org/10.3991/ijim.v17i07.37201

Dyer, K. M., & Carothers, J. (2000). *The intuitive principal: A guide to leadership.* Corwin Press.

Eynon, R., & Young, E. (2021). Methodology, legend, and rhetoric: The constructions of AI by academia, industry, and policy groups for lifelong learning. *Science, Technology, & Human Values, 46*(1), 166–191. https://doi.org/10.1177/0162243920906475

Fardouly, J., Magson, N. R., Johnco, C. J., Oar, E. L., & Rapee, R. M. (2018). Parental control of the time preadolescents spend on social media: Links with preadolescents' social media appearance comparisons and mental health. *Journal of Youth and Adolescence, 47*(7), 1456–1468. https://doi.org/10.1007/s10964-018-0870-1

Fenjiro, Y. (2023, April 17). ChatGPT & GPT 4, How it works? *Medium.* https://medium.com/@fenjiro/chatgpt-gpt-4-how-it-works-10b33fb3f12b

Forbes, A. (n.d.). *Six reasons every teacher needs to talk to students about AI.* MacQuarie University. https://d3c33hcgiwev3.cloudfront.net/GfvZ8JV2SMy72f

Garcia, M. (2016). Racist in the machine: The disturbing implications of algorithmic bias. *World Policy Journal, 33*(4), 111–117.

Glassman, J., Humphreys, K., Yeung, S., Smith, M., Jauregui, A., Milstein, A., & Sanders, L. (2021). Parents' perspectives on using artificial intelligence to reduce technology interference during early childhood: Cross-sectional online survey. *Journal of Medical Internet Research, 23*(3), e19461. https://doi.org/10.2196/19461

Hart, W. H. (2018). Is it rational or intuitive? Factors and processes affecting school superintendents' decisions when facing professional dilemmas. *Educational leadership and administration: Teaching and Program Development, 29*(1), 14–25.

Holmes, W., & Porayska-Pomsta, K. (Eds.). (2023). *The ethics of artificial intelligence in education: Practices, challenges, and debates.* Routledge. https://doi.org/10.4324/9780429329067

ILO Group. (2024). *Framework for implementing artificial intelligence in K-12 education.* ILO Group. https://www.ilogroup.com/wp-content/uploads/2024/03/Printable-Framework-for-Implementing-Artificial-Intelligence-AI-in-K-12-Education_v1.0.pdf

Impact Research. (2023). *Understanding teacher and student views on ChatGPT*. Walton Family Foundation. https://www.waltonfamilyfoundation. org/understanding-teacher-and-student-views-on-chatgpt

Kabakci Yurdakul, I., Odabasi, H. F., Kilicer, K., Coklar, A. N., Birinci, G., & Kurt, A. A. (2012). The development, validity and reliability of TPACK-deep: A technological pedagogical content knowledge scale. *Computers & Education, 58*(3), 964–977. https://doi.org/10.1016/j.compedu.2011.10.012

Kliebard, H. M. (2004). *The struggle for the American curriculum, 1893–1958* (3rd ed.). Routledge.

Kong, S.-C. (2018). Parents' perceptions of e-learning in school education: Implications for the partnership between schools and parents. *Technology, Pedagogy and Education, 27*(1), 15–31. https://doi.org/10.1080/1475939X.2017.1317659

Lesiv, A.-S. (2023, March 20). The acceleration of artificial intelligence. *Contrary*. https://www.contrary.com/foundations-and-frontiers/ai-acceleration

Lin, L. (2024, May 15). A quarter of U.S. teachers say AI tools do more harm than good in K-12 education. *Pew Research Center*. https://www.pewresearch. org/short-reads/2024/05/15/a-quarter-of-u-s-teachers-say-ai-tools-do-more-harm-than-good-in-k-12-education/

Luckin, R., Holmes, W., Griffiths, M., & Forcier, L. B. (2016). *Intelligence unleashed: An argument for AI in education*. UCL Knowledge Lab. https://www.pearson.com/content/dam/corporate/global/pearson-dot-com/files/innovation/Intelligence-Unleashed-Publication.pdf

Martinez, M. (2023). *Personal communication*.

MathWorks. (2024, April 3). *Nearly half high school students say generative AI will significantly change the future workforce, global survey reveals*. MathWorks Math Modeling Challenge. https://m3challenge.siam.org/newsroom/high-school-student-survey-generative-ai/

Mishra, P., & Koehler, M. J. (2006). Technological pedagogical content knowledge: A framework for integrating technology in teachers' knowledge. *Teachers College Record, 108*(6), 1017–1054.

Morgan, H. (2021). Howard Gardner's multiple intelligences theory and his ideas on promoting creativity. In F. Reisman (Ed.), *Celebrating giants and trailblazers: A-Z of who's who in creativity research and related fields*. KIE Publications. https://aquila.usm.edu/fac_pubs/19828

Nava, M. (2023). *Personal communication*.

Ng, D. T. K., Leung, J. K. L., Su, M. J., Yim, I. H. Y., Qiao, M. S., & Chu, S. K. W. (2022). *AI literacy in K-16 classrooms*. Springer International Publishing. https://doi.org/10.1007/978-3-031-18880-0_1

NPBEA, National Policy Board for Educational Administration. (2015). *Professional standards for educational leaders*. https://www.npbea.org/wp-content/uploads/2017/06/Professional-Standards-for-Educational-Leaders_2015.pdf

O'Brien, M. (2023, August 1). Chatbots sometimes make things up. Is AI's hallucination problem fixable? *AP News.* https://apnews.com/article/artificial-intelligence-hallucination-chatbots-chatgpt-falsehoods-ac4672c5b06e6f91050aa46ee731bcf4

OECD. (2024). *Recommendation of the Council on Artificial Intelligence.* OECD Legal Instruments. https://legalinstruments.oecd.org/en/instruments/OECD-LEGAL-0449

Ouyang, F., & Jiao, P. (2021). Artificial intelligence in education: The three paradigms. *Computers and Education: Artificial Intelligence, 2,* 100020. https://doi.org/10.1016/j.caeai.2021.100020

Pahl, S. (2023, February 16). An emerging divide: Who is benefiting from AI?. *Industrial Analytics Platform.* https://iap.unido.org/articles/emerging-divide-who-benefiting-ai

Ramírez-Rueda, M. del C., Cózar-Gutiérrez, R., Roblizo Colmenero, M. J., & González-Calero, J. A. (2021). Towards a coordinated vision of ICT in education: A comparative analysis of Preschool and Primary Education teachers' and parents' perceptions. *Teaching and Teacher Education, 100,* 103300. https://doi.org/10.1016/j.tate.2021.103300

Riddell, R. (2024, May 3). Ed tech venture funding hit lowest point in a decade in Q1 2024. *K-12 Dive.* https://www.k12dive.com/news/ed-tech-venture-funding-lowest-point-since-2014-q1-2024/715093/

Ruiz, R. (2024, April 30). Explicit deepfakes in school: How to protect students. *Mashable.* https://mashable.com/article/deepfakes-of-students-in-school

Sidoti, O., & Gottfried, J. (2023, November 16). About 1 in 5 U.S. teens who've heard of ChatGPT have used it for schoolwork. *Pew Research Center.* https://www.pewresearch.org/short-reads/2023/11/16/about-1-in-5-us-teens-whove-heard-of-chatgpt-have-used-it-for-schoolwork/

Stahl, B. C., Schroeder, D., & Rodrigues, R. (2023). *Ethics of artificial intelligence: Case studies and options for addressing ethical challenges.* Springer International Publishing. https://doi.org/10.1007/978-3-031-17040-9

Touretzky, D., Gardner-McCune, C., Martin, F., & Seehorn, D. (2019). Envisioning AI for K-12: what should every child know about AI? *Proceedings of the AAAI Conference on Artificial Intelligence, 33*(01), Article 01. https://doi.org/10.1609/aaai.v33i01.33019795

Tsuei, M., & Hsu, Y.-Y. (2019). Parents' acceptance of participation in the integration of technology into children's instruction. *The Asia-Pacific Education Researcher, 28*(5), 457–467. https://doi.org/10.1007/s40299-019-00447-3

Turk, V. (2023, October 10). How AI reduces the world to stereotypes. *Rest of World.* https://restofworld.org/2023/ai-image-stereotypes/

U.S. Department of Education, Office of Educational Technology. (2023). *Artificial intelligence and future of teaching and learning: Insights and recommendations.* https://tech.ed.gov/ai/

UNICEF. (2021). *Policy guidance on AI for children.* United Nations Children's Fund (UNICEF). www.unicef.org/globalinsight/media/2356/file/UNICEF-Global-Insight-policy-guidance-AI-children-2.0-2021.pdf

Vincent, J. (2019, December 11). Why are so many AI systems named after Muppets? *The Verge.* https://www.theverge.com/2019/12/11/20993407/ai-language-models-muppets-sesame-street-muppetware-elmo-bert-ernie

Westrope. (2023, November 29). CITE23: AI tools raise new legal questions for K-12. *GovTech.* https://www.govtech.com/education/k-12/cite23-ai-tools-raise-new-legal-questions-for-k-12

Williamson, B. (2021). Meta-edtech. *Learning, Media and Technology, 46*(1), 1–5. https://doi.org/10.1080/17439884.2021.1876089

Wright, M. (2023). *Personal communication.*

CHAPTER 3

Artificial Intelligence and Changing the Arc of Education

Abstract This chapter examines how artificial intelligence (AI) is changing the arc of education. We address common concerns of educational leaders, such as inclusivity and efficacy, and the impact of AI applications on these concerns. We concentrate on how the AI revolution is shaping and will continue to shape how educational leaders address these concerns while still centering student needs. This chapter extends the general information from the previous chapter to include more specific examples of applications that are changing what is happening in classrooms and schools. This chapter is most concerned with implementation, discussing what teachers and educational leaders can do with AI (i.e., lesson planning, predictive assessments), and the implications of these new powers (i.e., policies, data management).

Keywords Artificial intelligence in education (AIED) • Chatbots • Accessibility • Educational assessment • Efficacy • Standards • Policy

This chapter looks at the question of how artificial intelligence (AI) is changing the arc of education. We address common concerns of educational leaders, such as inclusivity and efficacy, and the impact of AI applications on these concerns. We concentrate on how the AI revolution is changing and will continue to shape the ways educational leaders address

K. Moran Jackson, R. Papa, *AI Changing the Arc of Educational Leadership*, https://doi.org/10.1007/978-3-031-71415-3_3

these concerns, while still centering student needs. Chapter 2 extends the general information from the first chapter to more specific examples of applications that are changing what is happening in classrooms and schools. This chapter is most concerned with implementation, discussing what teachers and educational leaders can do with AI (i.e., lesson planning, predictive assessments) as well as the implications of these new powers (i.e., policies, data management).

GENERATION: TEACHING THOUGHTFUL INQUIRY

The most buzz regarding AI applications in education surrounds the explosive development of chatbots. The first chatbots date to the 1960s when computer programs were tested as assistants for psychotherapy (Adiguzel et al., 2023; Labadze et al., 2023). Using rules-based programs, the older style of chatbot could offer predetermined responses to choices selected by users in an attempt to "simulate a conversation interaction between the user and a computer, using natural language" (Yang & Evans, 2020). Chatbots now have the same goal but with more advanced programming. Based on natural language processing (NLP) and deep learning, chatbots no longer rely on pre-scripted responses (Huang, 2023). AI chatbots now can generate novel responses to novel user input. The chatbots can produce text responses ranging from narratives to computer code to translations, with some models also able to produce novel visual outputs (Rudolph et al., 2023, p. 344). Because these chatbots generate new material, they fall under the umbrella of generative AI.

In both traditional and social media platforms, there is much discussion about the use of generative AI programs for cheating in education (Coffey, 2024; Eke, 2023; Roose, 2023). With the responses generated by AI chatbots so natural, students will (and have) used the applications to write essays, discussion posts, and other material used in schools both for communication and assessment. In response, schools are using other AI applications to try and catch cheaters by evaluating the likelihood that a piece of writing was generated by an AI. This has led to the development of other AI applications designed to make AI generated text more natural sounding. This has led to the creation of more AI detection software and attempts to watermark AI output. As with historical attempts to guard against cheating in schools, there is an endless cycle.

AI chatbots are commonly used for homework help, personalization of learning, and skill development (Labadze et al., 2023). Students who use chatbots reported that they liked the quick responses, the ability to naturally interact, and the ability to offer additional resources offered by the technology (Chen et al., 2023). Students also noted that they liked being able to ask questions of the chatbot "without revealing what they know (or don't know) to the course instructor" (Chen et al., 2023, p. 168).

The most commonly cited problems with chatbots arise as with other AI platforms regarding student privacy and data permissions (Okonkwo & Ade-Ibijola, 2021). However, there are growing concerns with the efficacy of chatbots versus other teaching and learning options, with the newness of the medium impacting a lack of capacity development among educators to assess its true educational value (Eke, 2023). Despite these concerns, the use of chatbots in education will continue to grow (Latif et al., 2023), especially as more technology platforms used in schools add chatbot capabilities to their services.

For example, in January 2024, Microsoft made its chatbot, Copilot, available to educators and higher education students using the operating system, Microsoft 365 (Government Technology, 2024). The enterprise version of Microsoft 365 is commonly used in schools and districts and has built-in several security and privacy features that comply with existing regulations. The new chatbot is also coupled with other services such as an AI learning path on its professional development site and apps that allow for personalization of reading exercises. In January 2024, Google announced more integration of AI within Google classrooms, including AI-generated questions aligned with timestamps in YouTube videos and assigning personalized readings for differentiation of individuals or groups (Wallen, 2024). Across systems, educators will increasingly see AI programs integrated within their Learning Management Systems (LMSs) and associated systems.

With the growth in access to chatbots, we also will see growth in how chatbots are used outside of low-stakes applications of student engagement or practice problems (Adiguzel et al., 2023). One way that chatbots are increasingly used in assessments is through taking on teacher workloads. Teachers can use chatbots to help develop assessment items, generate rubrics, and assist in the evaluation of student work (Herft, 2023; Latif et al., 2023; Okonkwo & Ade-Ibijola, 2021). Chatbots can also be used administratively, as assistants for student services, assessment scoring, and scheduling tasks (Latif et al., 2023; Okonkwo & Ade-Ibijola, 2021).

Educators are also using generative AI applications to create teaching materials, assessments, and other resources. Celik et al. (2022) found that AI applications could assist teachers with planning, class materials and directions, and assessments. One study found that for teachers across eastern China, the more they knew about AI, the less threatened they felt about the implications of AI for education (Wang et al., 2023). The authors of the study also noted that with the increasing pace of technological advancement in AI, it would be impossible for teachers to learn about these aspects of applications. Rather teaching development should focus on "adequate knowledge, skills, and vision as well as ethics, that is, AI readiness, so as to make informed decisions about what AI to use and how to use AI appropriately" (Wang et al., 2023, p. 10).

Many of the generative AI applications, building on a vast trove of previously published examples, can create lesson plans, essential questions, worksheets, leveled readings, web quests, and a myriad of other materials used by teachers and students. Some companies cater to teachers by offering suites of AI tools used to generate class materials. Some popular programs such as MagicSchool.ai and Learnt.ai are generally designed with pretrained AI assistants to help with lesson plans, Independent Educational Programs (IEPs), emails, and other materials teachers need to create for their classes. The output of these programs can often integrate with other educational software, such as Google Classroom. Other companies specialize in providing materials for teachers within subject areas, such as Twee for English language arts teachers. Teachers using these AI platforms need to be concerned with the cost of accessing these programs, the ability of these programs to maintain student privacy conventions, and the accessibility of applications for all students.

In addition to chatbots and AI-integrated assistants, other AI applications are also finding their way into schools. One area of increasing growth for AI is wearable technology. Citing Rao, Borthwick et al. (2015) describe wearable technology as "digital devices or computers that can be worn and used in the real world (Rao, 2014)" (p. 85), noting that calculator watches were the first incarnation. They go on to note that wearable technology offers advantages for student engagement and accessibility for students with disabilities. However, these devices suffer from similar problems to other AI applications in terms of securing student privacy and equity of access. Educators familiar with the abilities of these wearable technologies appreciate the pedagogical uses, such as the ability of students to engage in simulations and instant feedback, but worry about logistical and quality concerns, such as overall cost and overreliance (Bower & Sturman, 2015).

Virtual reality headsets fit within this category of wearable devices. These headsets immerse the wearer in a simulated world that allows for some degree of interaction (Stein, 2024). While headsets are the most popular way to engage with virtual reality, the Institute of Electrical and Electronics

Engineers (IEEE) uses the term XR to encompass VR, AR, and spatial computing (Fox & Thornton, 2022). All of these technologies involve the heavy use of AI technology and other computing techniques for the prediction and generation required to create pictures and depict actions in a virtual world. These tools allow for the user to be involved in a real, physical space while also interacting with an overlapping virtual space. Many major technology companies are developing these wearable devices. The Vision Pro was released by Apple in early 2024, with Samsung and Google also set to release updated versions of their XR-enabled products soon after.

The opportunity for AI-enhanced devices to increase accessibility for students is a key factor driving their use. Xie et al. (2019) stated, "We believe that the popularity of wearable learning technologies with personalized data will be a new trend in adaptive/personalized learning" (p. 13). A public university professor of technology discussed the kinds of questions educators need to ask about technology and accessibility:

> *This comes back to … this idea of inclusivity and usability. … I think that we need to think about, does this meet the needs of the economically disadvantaged? Does this meet the needs of those who have health issues of some sort or another, those who are not located within a hub of space where they can be? And of course, being the father of a child with a cognitive disability, Does this meet the needs of individuals with disabilities? It does support them in growing, right? Because if the tool is so limited, that it only supports wealthy white kids, we've got a real problem. And that's where it starts, we kind of know that, because those are the people that are designing them. … We need to be thinking about all of those other populations. And I know I only included a few.* (Armfield, 2023)

IEEE outlined several challenges surrounding XR and accessibility including: (1) the centering of some experiences as the norm versus a more individualized experience, (2) the building on work and experiences of users without credit or compensation given to individuals, (3) the misuse of designs intended for prosocial experiences, and (4) the collection of large amounts of personal data, including biological data such as hearth rate or eye-tracking, without clear uses for such data. They also list several options for technology to implement to increase accessibility depending on the nature of a student's disability. For example, for students who need accommodations for vision, the XR app should be able to: alter the size of objects and text, transform text to speech, apply color filters, or adjust background elements to increase readability. Buyers of these technologies in schools are advised to check the ability of the applications to perform these basic functions of inclusivity.

The ability of these applications to personalize learning and address accessibility continues to excite educators, and for good reason. In an interview with a large urban public school Central Office Administrator, they discussed the excitement that educators felt about the ability to reach students with generative AI applications:

> *I was doing a workshop with leaders from around the state, and we were talking about our emergent bilinguals, or English learners. … We don't have enough people that can serve as interpreters. So if AI can help get those ideas that our students are sharing, in a way that the teacher can understand that, I think that would be very beneficial. … We have an over-referral of English learners, or special education, because a lot of times they're taking in all of that information, and they're not ready to produce in their second language. This [AI application] might be helpful in reducing the number of referrals, because now teachers will say, "The student is fully capable, they just need more time." And this is a tool that's helping them get their ideas onto the screen. … What that would do is actually free up resources that now our psychologist doesn't have to engage in testing for students that really should not have been referred in the first place.* (Nava, 2023)

Speaking specifically to the needs of a multilingual, multicultural student community, Wang et al. (2023) stated:

> It is vital to recognize that AI is not a one-size-fits-all solution and should be implemented in ways that align with international students' unique needs and cultural differences. … Ultimately, institutions should view AI in education as a tool that enhances the important role of human educators in supporting and guiding international students throughout their academic journeys. (Wang et al., 2023, p. 10)

Yet we also need to be concerned with how these new devices are manifested. Does access to these enhancements become mandatory, or is access restricted, as it is currently, to the few people who already deal in abundance? AI ethicists are rightly concerned with the ultimate possibilities of enhanced human beings. Bostrom (2017) termed this possibility transhumanism: a continuum of augmenting humans by means of AI and other technological alterations. For example, now we treat vision problems with glasses, contact lenses, or laser eye surgery, but in the future technology might allow fixes beyond the normal 20/20 and add binocular or night vision (UK Department of Defence, 2021).

Assessment: Finding Compatibility

AI has been in the background of educational assessments for several years. Some curriculum suppliers have been leaning on techniques of machine learning to create personalized practice and assessment items for students. For over a decade, large-scale assessments (LSAs) have used advanced statistical and computer programming to identify assessment item difficulty (hard questions versus easy questions), to feed appropriately leveled questions to students, and use student performance on these questions to generate scores or levels of achievement (Okubo et al., 2023). These computer-aided tests are generally based on techniques such as item response theory which allow items to be rated at a particular difficulty level. Then, student performance on different levels of items allows for an algorithmic determination of ability. There is considerable support for these techniques compared to the standard assessments that simply count the number of right or wrong without considering item difficulty (Mujtaba & Mahapatra, 2020).

AI assessment tools are leveling up computer-adapted tests (CATs) by including machine learning and personalization (Mujtaba & Mahapatra, 2020). Rather than relying on a programmed path through the items, CATs can use algorithms based on previous data and compare that to ongoing student performance. In this way, real-time information from the students is used to choose the next most appropriate item to estimate content knowledge. Consequently, two students taking the same test may not see the same set of questions. This lack of standardization in questions might at first be problematic for some educators, but alternative form tests have been around and validated for years (Clarke & Luna-Bazaldua, 2021).

The generative aspect of these AI assessment tools is seen as a distinct advantage over traditional assessment tools (Choi, 2020). More advanced versions of the AI assessment tools will also be able to create new practice problems and assessment items based on the framework from previous items. This would allow students who need reinforcement of content to have an almost unlimited number of practice problems, working with a machine that will never tire from giving accurate and encouraging feedback. AI has grown the programs that are measured and used for school achievement assessment. According to Saltman, this approach serves the universal objective knowledge which means "tests obscure the cultural politics of knowledge that informs the selection of knowledge to be taught, and they circumscribe the range of possible interpretations and interpretive frameworks for claims to truth" (2022, p. 31).

Another current problem with AI assessment tools is the difficulty of grading open-response items such as essays, posters, or other student-created items (Rudolph et al., 2023). For example, a study by Khademi (2023) found that compared to experienced human raters, two popular AI chatbots (Open AI's ChatGPT and Google's Bard) could not as effectively identify the complexity level of writing prompts for an assessment. The authors cautioned against using chatbots for applications such as "translation, automated essay scoring, and automated item generation" (p. 8). This concern with AI being used by students for assessments was noted by a large urban public school Central Office Administrator:

> So, I think right now, the debate that we're having in the district and it's an emerging one is, what would we accept in terms of student work that they've provided with us? And then what would we not accept? What would we reject? And the other is how do we know when they are using AI tools? I think in some instances, it might be very easy to tell, just based on previous work that has been submitted from students, but then the other is, how will we really know and be certain? Because if we're staking a grade on this pass, or no pass, we have to be absolutely sure. (Nava, 2023)

AI use in assessment will likely only become more common (Adiguzel et al., 2023) and some argue that using chatbots in assessment can allow for the evaluation of higher-order thinking skills as it allows for conversations (Ifelebuegu et al., 2023). Assessment developers can and will use more specialized AI models to address problems with item development, selection, and scoring (Mujtaba & Mahapatra, 2020). For example, Preston and Salman (2024) reported that the developers of the PISA exam, an international assessment of the world's 15-year-olds, are planning to use AI to help design the test in 2029. PISA's discussion includes how AI can help in designing and scoring personalized tests, specific to the home context of students. Another way that AI will impact international tests is through the inclusion of student AI content knowledge such as how to use and evaluate AI materials.

The growing use of AI applications to develop and grade assessments is causing a wide re-evaluation of how assessments are used in schools. Compton succinctly summarized up this re-evaluation by asking, "If an essay produced by ChatGPT can pass our assessments, doesn't that suggest a potential flaw in the assessment itself? Shouldn't our assignments require more critical thinking, originality and/or use of appropriate scholarship than a current AI tool can generate?" (n.d., p. 2). Educators would likely agree that most assignments and assessments should require higher-level skills as these are more often the skills we are seeking to develop in our students. However, we sometimes do need to assess rote skills, especially with our younger students or those new to a content field.

AI systems will become increasingly sophisticated, and the need to constantly recreate AI-resilient assessments may be a fatalistic task. Perhaps, the change needs to come in how we approach the reasoning behind the assessment. So much of assessment work is geared toward accountability, either to enforce teaching quality or to enforce gradations of student learning. Rather if assessment is viewed as a tool for student feedback and development, with or without the aid of AI, the feedback will be more authentic to student needs.

In the case study that frames this chapter, we address two problems that result from AI applications in school: implementation and policies. First, with access to AI applications growing, not only students but also educators will find growing uses for these tools. These uses may or may not align with the educational values and goals of other stakeholders, leading to conflicts. Potential conflicts in applications lead to the second issue, the creation of AI policies. With the fast pace of growth for AI applications in education, policy will have a hard time keeping up with new uses, a concern we cover later in the chapter.

Case Study #2
Part A
The principal of a high school received an email from a parent. In the email, the parent explained that while reviewing homework with their student, they learned that a social studies teacher was using an AI application to help grade students. The parent was very upset that students were not receiving individual feedback from teachers. They

(*continued*)

(continued)

were also worried about the amount of oversight for the program—how could they be sure their child was receiving a fair grade? The parent's email clearly stated that they did not want "a computer to be grading my child" and they asked for a meeting with the teacher and principal.

The principal forwarded the note to the teacher asking to speak with them during their prep period. During the meeting, the teacher explained that they use AI to help grade the essay answers on reading quizzes based on the textbook. Students were using a form imported into the LMS that collects both multiple-choice and short-answer questions. The format was similar to the quiz function in the LMS. The difference was that the teacher exported the answers from the LMS into an AI program that the teacher had prepped with answers to the quiz, including an example of an "expert" answer to the essay question, based on answers the teacher had seen in previous years. The AI was then able to assign a score of 1–5 to the student essays based on how similar they were to the example answer.

The teacher explained that computers have been automatically grading multiple-choice and short answer questions for years. The addition of grading a short essay question seemed like a minor issue especially since the essay was only 5 points out of 20 on the weekly, open-note quiz. The teacher also noted that they did review responses when they saw grades that were unusual compared to students' previous performance, but they had not found any issues with the program. The teacher argued that having the AI application grade the essay was saving them more than two hours every week and that they were able to use that time to plan more effective lessons.

What do you identify as the cause of this problem? Are there possible other causes?

Identify at least three possible solutions to this problem. What would be some possible impacts of each of these solutions on stakeholders?

As the principal in this case, what would be your next steps to gather more information and remain curious about this problem?

ADAPTATION: CO-OPTING AI

In our discussions with educational leaders, we have found that educators tend to approach AI use in classrooms in one of four ways. First, some choose to *ban* AI applications entirely. Second, they may choose to *police* the applications. In these cases, educators establish clear rules for when AI applications can and cannot be used, and these rules are accompanied by clear consequences for violations of the rules. Many of the policy recommendations discussed later in the chapter fall under one of these two responses.

A third response is that educators can *teach* the applications. Educators making this choice include AI applications and content within their curriculum, concentrating on working with students to understand how the applications can be used responsibly. In these classrooms and schools, rules regarding appropriate use and possible consequences for misuse are often less clear. There is the potential, therefore, of allowing for more misuse. However, there is also the possibility of more knowledge growth and development through the autonomy students and teachers are given. A large urban school district administrator described what they see regarding teacher and students learning about AI together:

> *I think AI is a good tool. But it doesn't work just as, "Here do this." ... It's way more effective when teachers are engaged and are monitoring the students' progress and providing encouragement and connections support along the way. Just as I think it's probably true with any tool. And to step back and or even try to learn how to use it appropriately that there's a lot of resistance to it. But AI is here to stay. And so what we're hoping to do, within our approach ... we want to build some knowledge and literacy and acceptance of it, like, "Hey, this is a tool."* (Nava, 2023)

Of equal note from the perspective of a public urban university technologist with school age children:

> *The key is to encourage kids to ask why an AI came up with a given answer and see if the kids can understand the process. This is so much more important since AI tools can also help teachers know work was created by an AI.* (Martinez, 2023)

A natural extension of the third option is the fourth approach to AI use in classrooms. The last approach is to *co-opt* the applications, using them in new and inventive ways that take students beyond initial, perhaps limited, use cases. Tapping into student and teacher autonomy and creativity, co-opting AI centers student and educator needs, not the vision of the designer. Even well-designed programs cannot anticipate every child's need in every classroom. Co-opting an application allows the human to make the decision of need and use. A public urban university technologist discussed the advantages of this type of approach:

> *I am looking for educational institutions to help students to be able to question/ process and ultimately be able to question/query AI systems. In other words, co-opt AI use by students to benefit students. It becomes efficient when education focuses on how to use AI for the purpose of teaching and learning instead of looking at it as a threat that isn't useful and that can harm students by developing anti-AI learning/teaching policies.* (Martinez, 2023)

The desire to be creative in education comes not only from teachers, but also from our social expectations for students. Schools are expected to teach students beyond simple academic content to twenty-first century skills, social-emotional learning, and professional skills. Teaching these types of goals requires more than standard content presentation through lectures and readings, followed by standardized assessments. Although standardized testing continues to hold many schools in thrall, the increasing recognition of the need to teach higher level competencies means that we need school applications that go beyond content presentation. The creativity of educators, combined with student interest and administrative support, has already shown how some schools are capable of reaching these goals with access to non-AI powered computer applications and textbooks.

What will the future look like if we are able to encourage our educators to work with AI for the same ultimate goal? Can we give educators this freedom to co-opt the app, to center the human in the application, or will they instead be forced to follow the needs of the machine? While co-opting an AI application has the goal of making an AI application work for student benefit, there is a need to question why the applications need to be co-opted at all. Shouldn't the point of AI applications used in education be to help students in the first place? Traditionally, something is co-opted when it is working at cross-purposes to you or when it is not designed to be aligned with your values. While overall the potential of AI applications in schools is high, educators need to remain aware that the motives of the developers or creators might not be the same as theirs. Consequently, developers should be aware that educators can rightly mistrust these systems.

EFFICACY: USING TO ONE'S CAPACITY

Whether an educator decides to use an AI application in classes or encourages their students to do so is likely linked to their efficacy in using the application. Self-efficacy, or the self-belief in one's ability to perform a behavior, is linked to both teacher and student behaviors in classrooms (Lazarides & Warner, 2020). To increase self-efficacy in a field, people depend on four inputs: experience, role modeling, persuasion from others, and emotions. If an educator can build personal experience using an application, if they watch someone else use the application successfully, if they are told about the positive benefits of using the application, or if they have a personal interest and positive view toward the application, the educator is more likely to use the application, and use it successfully.

Theoretically, this shows the importance of well-organized and well-run professional development on AI for educators (Teach AI, 2023). In addition to knowledge building, educators need these experiences to feel confident embarking on AI use in the classroom. A large urban public school central office administrator had this to say about professional development in AI:

> I think if we had professional development, some kind of training, more real life kind of instances of how this is being used or applied. I think it would be very useful to our senior leadership, to our school leaders, and then to our faculty, our educators, our teachers. I would say right now there isn't there's an awareness of it. And even with colleagues that I've spoken to the ones who have shared that they've interacted with some of these tools, it's been more of an exploratory curiosity type. There's very little happening in terms of people using it intentionally as a tool, whether it's for curriculum, whether it's for lesson plan, design. It's very superficial right now. And I think part of it is just this lack of awareness of what it really is. And I think the more that we learn about that, then we'd be able to incorporate it more. (Nava, 2023)

Self-efficacy is an individual variable and all educators are individuals with their own backgrounds and emotional responses. Sitting in the same professional development session will not guarantee the same results. According to Rogers' theory of technology adaptation (2003), we know that there are innovators and early adopters who will engage eagerly with new technology. These are the teachers and administrators who are already using AI applications in their work, helping their peers to find new tools and techniques, and perhaps even designing the professional development sessions we are discussing. The majority of educators will be deliberate in how they take up the applications over time, pushed by internal motivations, external mandates, and likely some degree of skepticism.

As in all things, there will be those who choose not to engage with this new technology in their work beyond requirements and perhaps even those reluctantly. A limited number of educators are likely to choose to only lightly or even never engage with AI materials beyond school or district mandates. This choice may have as much to do with individual preferences as efficacy or development. While we do not yet know what will drive the decision to not engage with AI, we know from studies of previous technology uptake that those who choose not to engage are typically traditional, hesitant to change in general, and distrustful of technology (Rogers, 2003).

How much educators and students should be forced to engage with these programs, even against their expressed desire, will be a matter of decision of educational leaders. We regularly make students engage in school activities against their wishes. Even now, not many of our students are overjoyed to solve a set of math problems. Will it matter if an AI controls the question sets on the computer screen? Will students or their parents be able to opt out of the use of such applications and for what reasons? Again, educational leaders will be confronted with wicked questions of action when making decisions not only about whether or which AI applications should be allowed in classrooms, but also about whether such use should be optional or required.

STANDARDS MANAGING PREPARATION

These questions about the use of AI applications are already finding their way into schools through curriculum. A rural public school Superintendent described this ongoing change and how their district manifested better use of AI through a new curriculum bound to standards teaching tied to AI tools:

> Last school year, we implemented a district wide curriculum K through 12 which incorporated within are some AI tools. And so what it's doing really, it's forcing the teacher's hand where they're having to align their instruction with standards, because the curriculum is aligned with the standards. So, it's really forcing teachers and I don't know of a better word, but it's really forcing them to use the AI tools because we're saying, Look, any curriculum, even if its average, and if it's implemented with fidelity, provided it is aligned with the standards,

you're going to see some outcome, you'll see student growth. And so, the reluctance [of some teachers] has been easier to overcome, because the same core of people that were pushing back on using these tools, were the ones that told me almost nine years ago, we don't have any curriculum we're having to use beyond textbooks. We don't have the support. Well, given that we spent nearly a million dollars, and it covers us for the next seven years to provide what they've been asking for. [And now we are saying] you've asked for this, and we've allowed you time to participate whether you did or you didn't that's up to you but time for discussion is over. Now we need to implement it. It's down to the administrative level, to the principal level, frankly, to ensure s/he looks at it during their [classroom] observations, seeing evidence of the incorporation of AI in our curriculum found in the daily lessons. What the [teachers] that have just dove into it and accepted it are finding, it's out of the box. If I were going back in the classroom, I was teaching English, I would be following it because it has worked. For me it has, you know, the questions to get you thinking. I think just change in general is what people struggle with. (Wright, 2023)

Twenty-first century school leaders are governed by standards for leadership preparation. Two professional organizations dominate the US professional code of standards and conduct of the school administrator. The American Association of School Administrators (AASA, 2023) provides the ethical code of conduct and the National Policy Board for Educational Administration (NPBEA, 2015) stipulates Professional Standards for Educational Leaders and the Interstate School Leaders Licensure Consortium (2015).

The American Association of School Administrators (AASA, 2023) offers the ethical code of behavior through "professional conduct towards (the community, professional associates, and students … increased student achievement and high expectations for each and every student" (p. 1). The Code of Ethics, adopted March 1, 2007, stated that an educational leader:

1. Makes the education and well-being of students the fundamental value of all decision making.
2. Fulfills all professional duties with honesty and integrity and always acts in a trustworthy and responsible manner.
3. Supports the principle of due process and protects the civil and human rights of all individuals.
4. Implements local, state and national laws.
5. Advises the school board and implements the board's policies and administrative rules and regulations.

6. Pursues appropriate measures to correct those laws, policies, and regulations that are not consistent with sound educational goals or that are not in the best interest of children.
7. Avoids using his/her position for personal gain through political, social, religious, economic or other influences.
8. Accepts academic degrees or professional certification only from accredited institutions.
9. Maintains the standards and seeks to improve the effectiveness of the profession through research and continuing professional development.
10. Honors all contracts until fulfillment, release or dissolution mutually agreed upon by all parties.
11. Accepts responsibility and accountability for one's own actions and behaviors.
12. Commits to serving others above self. (AASA, 2023, p. 1)

The National Policy Board for Educational Administration (NPBEA) offers professional standards for the practices and implementation derived from the AASA Code of Ethics. The NPBEA emphasizes school administrator performance-based approaches to evaluate the school principal and superintendent practices. Embedded in these standards is Standard 2. Ethics and Professional Norms (NPBEA, 2015) which states:

Effective educational leaders act ethically and according to professional norms to promote each student's academic success and well-being. Effective leaders: a) Act ethically and professionally in personal conduct, relationships with others, decision-making, stewardship of the school's resources, and all aspects of school leadership. b) Act according to and promote the professional norms of integrity, fairness, transparency, trust, collaboration, perseverance, learning, and continuous improvement. c) Place children at the center of education and accept responsibility for each student's academic success and well-being. d) Safeguard and promote the values of democracy, individual freedom and responsibility, equity, social justice, community, and diversity. e) Lead with interpersonal and communication skills, social-emotional insight, and understanding of all students' and staff members' backgrounds and cultures. f) Provide moral direction for the school and promote ethical and professional behavior among faculty and staff. (NPBEA, 2015, p. 16)

These broad national professional codes for ethical conduct by school administrators are taught in almost every university and college preparation program in the US whether they follow fully the tenets of AASA or

NPBEA. The Code of Ethics is found throughout the behavioral standards for the profession of school administration. An example of these concerns in real life was expressed by a large urban public school Central Office Administrator who discussed an ethical strategy toward the incorporation of AI tools into meeting the standards.

> *But I think the advice I'm just sharing with people who are in our professional development is don't necessarily push that technology away. We need to understand it so that we could better address it, you know, in our leadership and our preparation for it. Because I think sometimes educators tend to say it's a fad, or we don't need it. I've been teaching, you know, this way for 5, 10, 15 years and times change very quickly.* (Nava, 2023)

Professional standards and development go hand in hand. A public urban university Technologist described ethical use in the hands of professional organizations issuing standards, and the professional educators themselves. This strategy asks that it not be left to the curriculum companies.

> *If institutions focus on using AI to benefit teaching and learning, ethical questions become lessened by opportunities to encourage ethical use of the AI. Ethically it could have negative consequences for students as faculty begin to view AI use as a threat to their ability to lead teaching; but this could be minimized with proper professional development of faculty in navigating discipline specific uses of AI that could potentially enhance student learning.* (Martinez, 2023)

How educational leaders approach ethical issues and overlapping AI concerns in the future will be guided by both their professional development and the standards that oversee their work. However, training and standards can vary by context. Most states follow a code of conduct which is embedded in specific professional standards to measure practices that ensure ethical conduct. In a review of standards in three states (California, Florida, and Illinois) there were vast differences in the approaches a state takes toward educators, including positive language, negative *shall nots,* as well as legalese.

In the State of Florida, a school leader, in addition to striving to achieve the highest ethical conduct, must adhere to disciplinary principles under a strong threat of punishment. "Violation of any of these principles shall subject the individual to revocation or suspension of the individual educator's certificate, or the other penalties as provided by law" (Florida Department of Education, 2023). These principles translate into three categories of obligations for educators to the student, to the public, and to the profession. These obligations are most notably expressed in the negative including *shall not reasonably, shall not intentionally, shall not harass, exploit, violate,* and other negative phrases, in 12 out of the 14 stated obligations to students. For the obligations to the public, four out of five statements are in the negative. For the obligations to the profession, the obligations are equally negative in content.

In the State of Illinois, positive language was employed to encourage educators including school administrators, such as, *the individual should embody, respect, foster, assume responsibility, demonstrate, promote, support, collaborate,* and *aspire* (Illinois Code of Ethics, n.d., pp. 1–9). In California, professional standards frame the code of ethics for school administrators. The California approach also includes value expectations that translate into observable outcomes. Along with values such as those expressed in the Illinois code, specific actions are outlined in California's code to prove one's ability to lead a school.

> In California, the values are similar to professional organizations, the assessments beyond the legal ramifications for not doing positive ethical actions, are found embedded in Standard 3 Management of the Learning Environment which expects leaders to provide a safe learning through indicators such as "3A-3 Manage the acquisition, distribution, and maintenance of equipment, materials, and technology needed to meet the academic, linguistic, cultural, social-emotional, and physical requirements of students". (WestEd, 2016, p. 3)

Reflecting on the connection between implementation, standards, and teaching, a rural public school Superintendent said:

> *My perspective is an average curriculum implemented with fidelity that provides teachers tools are better than just allowing teachers to teach whatever we're going to teach and hope that it's aligned through their instruction with the standards and what students need ... We were lucky we had these funds because of COVID. We used them as a learning loss. Had we not had that influx of about five and a half million dollars, it never would have been attainable.* (Wright, 2023)

Providing a safe learning environment in the use of technology is expectedly impacted by national and state public policies. In this broader context, the digital divide and its relationship to inherent inequalities found in poverty are enormous concerns from the local to the global level. The gap between the affluent and those earning less within the world of AI has been and is continuing to exasperate the divide. The moral imperative between the nation state and the individual is often played out in punitive measures (i.e., Florida) for the individual educator. Clearly curriculum in its broadest sense must embrace student differences while seeking to mitigate privilege. Himma and Bottis (2014) remind us that "all technologies that resolve morally important problems take time to develop" (p. 343).

The professional organization International Society for Technology in Education's (ISTE) Standards for Education Leaders (2018) promotes technology guidance to school administrators. The standards promote the empowerment of the school leader to "3.b. Inspire a culture of innovation and collaboration that allows the time and space to explore and experiment with digital tools," [and] "support educators in using technology to advance learning that meets the diverse learning, cultural, and social-emotional needs of individual students" (p. 1). The way ISTE standards guide school leaders is not explicitly tied to the ethical actions required to assess educational tools. Rather the standards of practice expect the visionary planner to "2.c. Evaluate progress on the strategic plan, make course corrections, measure impact and scale effective approaches for using technology to transform learning" (p. 1).

Policy from the nation/state emanates from laws with the intention to correct educational practice. Policies are rarely proactive. Proactive leadership understands linkages from the law to district policy. A leader's role in this process must be guided by an ethical code of conduct approaching the "hows" and especially the "whys" to adopt and enforce.

POLICIES: BUILDING UP TO BEST USE

Policy development for school districts should both address AI tools in classrooms and ensure that the stakeholders understand ethical use of AI tools. Sandler (2014) offered an analysis for how to deal with emerging classroom tools that may broadly aid in curriculum development:

- Identify what are the benefits of the tool;
- Identify the legal/policy concerns;
- Identify who is empowered and who is potentially hurt or left out;
- Identify how the revised classroom curricular activities are affected; and,
- Rethink if it makes more curricular/teaching sense to not use the tool at all, such as, cultural differences are harmed, non-neutral gender, etc.

This approach overlaps with suggestions on how to approach wicked problems with an awareness of stakeholders and the impact of potential solutions. Doing so also requires time for deliberation and discussion, the features of remaining curious and gathering multiple viewpoints. A public urban university Technologist shared an exemplar of this approach toward support for faculty when considering policy:

> So, my job is to make sure we guide the discussion right now to recommend policy [working through the administration and the Faculty Senate] on professional development. However, I was able to convince administrators to not step into the policy issue yet before finishing three sessions [of professional development]. And the reason I I'd feel deeply about this, that I just, I'm a huge believer that once you set policy, it's really hard to walk it back. There is no better way to set policy than to wait out faculty concerns on potential use this tool in the classroom. Moving too quickly to recommend what the policies should be, [universities should not] charge along with any AI generated information, as long as you cite. In classrooms you can say less than 20% of the entire paper and you must cite it. Students need to know to say, "I got this from ChatGPT."
>
> We have so much that open AI and other companies are doing that is going to change anything you write now [specific policies] may not even be useful or fruitful or give faculty the tools they need to manage it in the near future. (Martinez, 2023)

Case Study #2
Part B
After meeting with the teacher, the principal reviewed the district policies regarding AI and found no explicit references to the use of AI for grading. The only references to AI prohibited student AI use for the creation of work products unless given explicit permission to use a specific program by a teacher. There were no restrictions given for teacher use.

What are the AI policies at your school or district or at a school or district you are familiar with? If you are not familiar with AI policies, some examples can be found at teachai.org/toolkit-guidance.

What are your feelings about policing AI use for students, but not for teachers? Do you think that is an effective compromise for districts to take? Why or why not?

With no policy either supporting or prohibiting teacher use of AI in this case, what options do the principal and the teacher have in response to the parent's concerns? What set of standards might help the principal think through options?

Most pre-K-12 school districts have ICT policies in place, even if loosely worded guidelines that resulted from the Covid-19 technological expansion. With AI applications now entering educational spaces, these policies may be questioned about their relevance. Most policies begin to "smell" after five years and should be regularly reviewed by the school board. Human beings are all about exceptions: administrators should consider wiggle room within policies with school rules that acknowledge the technological advancements that can and will render specific policies as faulty to implement. AI applications are in flux, so policies relating to them must also make room for flexibility. A university Professor of Technology offered another perspective on educational technology policies:

We have to make sure that our parents know what we're doing within the public schools. The more or the less abstract we are, the more forward we are with parents letting them know that we're going to be playing with these tools, we're going to be using these tools to help our students learn, we're going to be thinking about them, the better off we are. And even if that's just a line in an education technology policy that says AI tools will be used within these classrooms to support writing, to support thinking, and to support looking to see if I'm even cheating. You know those kinds of things come down to things like ChatGPT our students are using, regardless. So, helping them to think about if I use ChatGPT, what do I need to look for? What do I need to do in order to make sure that all that information that's pulled coming out of ChatGPT is correct? Because we know that even as good as it is right now, it doesn't clearly always hit all of the information correctly, right? I was watching a video about an individual who went back and took a class in high school, and they had to compare Ferris Bueller's Day Off *to something else and they misquoted. They quoted Ferris, and it should have been Ferris' best friend. So that kind of thing. You really got to make sure that our students are thinking about, "Oh, I can use it to support me and help me get things going. But what do I really need to do? And how do I need to think deeper through this?" I think that those are really important things and helping the parents understand that this is not the end all be all. This is just part of the learning process.* (Armfield, 2023)

Across the US, states are only now awaking to the good and bad of AI applications and their impacts on classrooms (Gallagher & Cottingham, 2023; Ghimire & Edwards, 2024). In the State of Virginia, their policy for faculty and staff focuses on the integrity found in honor codes and acceptable use practices while employing good human judgment.

1. Establish a culture of integrity: Define what this culture looks like (State Agencies and Governing Boards); Build a culture of integrity by discussing the honor code often with students and parents, implementing an honor code system with real consequences.
2. Follow an Acceptable Use Policy inside and outside the classroom: Codify Acceptable Use Policy (State Agencies/Governing Boards); Review and discuss the Acceptable Use Policy with students and parents (Faculty/Staff); Implement and hold learning community accountable for living up to Acceptable Use Policy.
3. Design assignments and assessments that encourage critical thinking and original thought and human judgement. (Commonwealth of Virginia, n.d., p. 4)

In California, there has been a specific insistence to create policy aimed at safeguarding children by enhancing media literacy. Implemented in January 2024, Assembly Bill 873 (2023–2024) stated the need for media literacy and expressed an intention to counter media influence in the state's classrooms:

(2) The growing ubiquity of new forms of media necessitates the need for comprehensive media literacy education for all elementary and secondary pupils.

(3) The State of California has a strong interest in ensuring that its pupils are equipped to confront questions about moral obligations and ethical standards regarding what appears on social media networks and digital platforms.

(4) The social implications of technological development are pervasive as over 90 percent of young adults use social media, and the reach and influence of digital media platforms will continue to expand.

(5) A Stanford University study showed that 82 percent of middle school pupils struggled to distinguish advertisements from news stories.

(6) The proliferation of online misinformation has posed risks to international peace, interfered with democratic decision-making, and threatened public health. (Assembly Bill No. 873 CHAPTER 815, 2023–2024).

The State of Washington Office of Public Instruction wrote to their state's policymakers a goal for AI in law with a focus on human agency.

Educational policymakers must focus on ensuring that the use of AI increases the public good, with emphasis on equity and inclusion. AI policy and use should be geared to improving learning for every student, empowering teachers, and strengthening learning management systems. It is important that policies also consider student safety and well-being and provide access to educational tools for all students. (Washington Office of Superintendent of Public Instruction, n.d., para. 9)

A large urban public school Central Office Administrator described the struggles that pre-K-12 schools and districts are facing regarding policy. Large-scale adoption of AI technologies are occurring through curriculum mandates enabled by significant increases in funding as noted earlier in this chapter by a rural public school superintendent. For a large urban multi-language district, it becomes equally critical to create flexible policies that allow for the use and sharing of that information with parents. Teachers also need professional development opportunities to become users of the technology. Additionally, professional organizations and state government educational support all must work together to create a synchronized approach.

Right now, what we're struggling with is something that we've struggled even beforehand where we have many teachers, a lot of our faculty, who tend to be sticklers for the rules. ... What I'm hearing from some of our principals that they're sharing is that teachers are adopting a zero tolerance policy if they find out that students are using AI tools to compose correctly or complete some of their assignments. Are they reading it, getting other things and putting those together? So, we're having a conversation where we're trying to bridge equitable grading with what they believe is fair and ethical. ... If a student has used AI tools, and you feel that they don't deserve a grade, that it isn't their original work, we can't just fail them or give them a zero. How are we going to use that critical grading? And in a sense, hold them accountable for their learning? So how do we turn around and use this as a learning tool? ... So, I think ethically, that's the conversation that we're having right now. And, of course, we have some of our teachers who are like, hey, they're being innovative, and they're using this tool, and they're submitting, and they're online searching, so it's really muddled right now. But it still kind of stems from a sense of a merit based type of completion of work or passing from one grade to the other. But I don't know if we really resolve that issue. And now when we're adding this other layer to it, I think it's becoming even more complicated. (Nava, 2023)

Case Study #2
Part C
The parent in the case above decided to speak at a board meeting about the use of AI to grade student assignments. In response to this discussion and media reports on AI, the board instructed the superintendent to develop a policy on AI that regulates student, teacher, and staff use. You, in your current role (teacher, teacher-in-training, educational leader, leader-in-training, parent, school or district staff member, etc.), are invited to be part of an advisory committee to work with the superintendent on creating this policy.

What practical considerations do you need to consider for the three groups targeted for policies? How do these considerations differ between the groups?

What are some of the implications of media and public perceptions on policy creation surrounding AI in schools?

Considering the changing nature of ed-tech and AI, how should the board and administrators evaluate the effectiveness of any policies they implement? How would groups best go about advocating for changes in the policy?

References

AASA. (2023). *AASA's statement of ethics for educational leaders.* https://www.aasa.org/docs/default-source/about/codeofethicsapprovedgb030107.pdf?sfvrsn=4bf2a388_2

Adiguzel, T., Kaya, M. H., & Cansu, F. K. (2023). Revolutionizing education with AI: Exploring the transformative potential of ChatGPT. *Contemporary Educational Technology, 15*(3), ep429. https://doi.org/10.30935/cedtech/13152

Armfield, S. (2023). *Personal communication.*

Borthwick, A. C., Anderson, C. L., Finsness, E. S., & Foulger, T. S. (2015). Special article personal wearable technologies in education: Value or villain? *Journal of Digital Learning in Teacher Education, 31*(3), 85–92. https://doi.org/10.1080/21532974.2015.1021982

Bostrom, N. (2017). *Superintelligence: Paths, dangers, strategies.* Oxford. ISBN 978-0-19-873983-8

Bower, M., & Sturman, D. (2015). What are the educational affordances of wearable technologies? *Computers & Education, 88*, 343–353. https://doi.org/10.1016/j.compedu.2015.07.013

Celik, I., Dindar, M., Muukkonen, H., & Järvelä, S. (2022). The promises and challenges of artificial intelligence for teachers: A systematic review of research. *TechTrends, 66*(4), 616–630. https://doi.org/10.1007/s11528-022-00715-y

Chen, Y., Jensen, S., Albert, L. J., Gupta, S., & Lee, T. (2023). Artificial intelligence (AI) student assistants in the classroom: Designing chatbots to support student success. *Information Systems Frontiers, 25*(1), 161–182. https://doi.org/10.1007/s10796-022-10291-4

Choi, J. (2020). Automatic item generation with machine learning techniques. A pathway to intelligent assessments. In J. Hong & R. Lissitz (Eds.), *Application of artificial intelligence to assessment*. IAP.

Clarke, M., & Luna-Bazaldua, D. (2021). *Primer on large-scale assessments of educational achievement*. The World Bank. https://documents.worldbank.org/en/publication/documents-reports/documentdetail/827991619500628075/Primer-on-Large-Scale-Assessments-of-Educational-Achievement

Coffey, L. (2024, February 9). Professors cautious of tools to detect AI-generated writing. *Inside Higher Ed.*. https://www.insidehighered.com/news/tech-innovation/artificial-intelligence/2024/02/09/professors-proceed-caution-using-ai

Commonwealth of Virginia. (n.d.). Guidelines for AI integration throughout education in the Commonwealth of Virginia. https://www.education.virginia.gov/media/governorvirginiagov/secretary-of-education/pdf/AI-Education-Guidelines.pdf

Compton, M. (n.d.). AI = Assessment Innovation. *Grow Beyond Grades*. https://growbeyondgrades.org/blog/ai-assessment-innovation

Eke, D. O. (2023). ChatGPT and the rise of generative AI: Threat to academic integrity? *Journal of Responsible Technology, 13*, 100060. https://doi.org/10.1016/j.jrt.2023.100060

Florida Department of Education. (2023). *Principles of professional conduct for the education profession in Florida: Rule 6A-10.081, Florida administrative code, principles of professional conduct for the education profession in Florida* (pp. 1–7). https://lcapst.org/training/4.9__The__Code__Of__Ethics__Of__The__Education__Profession__In__Flori.pdf

Fox, D., & Thornton, I. G. (2022). *The IEEE global initiative on ethics of extended reality (XR) report–Extended reality (XR) ethics and diversity, inclusion, and accessibility* (pp. 1–25). The Institute of Electrical and Electronics Engineers, Inc.. https://ieeexplore.ieee.org/abstract/document/9727122

Gallagher, H. A., & Cottingham, B. W. (2023, June 15). The urgent need to update district policies on student use of artificial intelligence in education. *Policy Analysis for California Education*. https://edpolicyinca.org/newsroom/urgent-need-update-district-policies-student-use-artificial-intelligence-education

Ghimire, A., & Edwards, J. (2024). From guidelines to governance: A study of AI policies in education. *ArXiv*. https://doi.org/10.48550/arXiv.2403.15601

Government Technology. (2024, January 30). Microsoft announces AI enhancements, tools for education. *GovTech*. https://www.govtech.com/education/higher-ed/microsoft-announces-ai-enhancements-tools-for-education

Herft, A. (2023). *A teacher's prompt guide to ChatGPT aligned with 'What Works Best'*. HerftEducator. https://www.canva.com/design/DAFW8z-D60c/ikjg6jQju5IRaseV6Izzcw/view?utm_content=DAFW8z-D60c&utm_campaign=designshare&utm_medium=link&utm_source=publishsharelink

Himma, K., & Bottis, M. (2014). The digital divide: Information technologies and the obligation to alleviate poverty. In R. L. Sandler (Ed.), *Ethics and emerging technologies* (pp. 333–362). Palgrave Macmillan. https://doi.org/10.1057/9781137349088

Huang, K. (2023, January 18). Alarmed by A.I. chatbots, universities start revamping how they teach. *The New York Times, International Edition*. https://www.proquest.com/docview/2766885034/citation/30EC3A82EB184DB1PQ/1

Ifelebuegu, A. O. (2023). Rethinking online assessment strategies: Authenticity versus AI chatbot intervention. *Journal of Applied Learning & Teaching*, 6(2). https://doi.org/10.37074/jalt.2023.6.2.2

Illinois Code of Ethics. (n.d.). *Illinois code of ethics*. pp. 1–9. https://www.isbe.net/Documents/educator_COE_0311.pdf

ISLLC—Interstate School Leaders Licensure Consortium 9. (2015). https://rsu23.org/wp-content/uploads/2018/03/GCOC-E1-ISLLC-Standards-3.pdf

Khademi, A. (2023). Can ChatGPT and Bard generate aligned assessment items? A reliability analysis against human performance. *Journal of Applied Learning & Teaching*, 6(1). https://doi.org/10.37074/jalt.2023.6.1.28

Labadze, L., Grigolia, M., & Machaidze, L. (2023). Role of AI chatbots in education: Systematic literature review. *International Journal of Educational Technology in Higher Education*, 20(1), 56. https://doi.org/10.1186/s41239-023-00426-1

Latif, E., Mai, G., Nyaaba, M., Wu, X., Liu, N., Lu, G., Li, S., Liu, T., & Zhai, X. (2023). AGI: Artificial general intelligence for education. *ArXiv*. https://doi.org/10.48550/arXiv.2304.12479

Lazarides, R., & Warner, L. M. (2020). Teacher self-efficacy. *Oxford Research Encyclopedia of Education*. https://doi.org/10.1093/acrefore/9780190264093.013.890

Martinez, M. (2023). *Personal communication*.

Mujtaba, D. F., & Mahapatra, N. R. (2020). Artificial intelligence in computerized adaptive testing. In *Proceedings of the 2020 International Conference on Computational Science and Computational Intelligence (CSCI)* (pp. 649–654). https://doi.org/10.1109/CSCI51800.2020.00116

Nava, M. (2023). *Personal communication.*

NPBEA, National Policy Board for Educational Administration (2015). *Professional standards for educational leaders.* https://www.npbea.org/wp-content/uploads/2017/06/Professional-Standards-for-Educational-Leaders_2015.pdf

Okonkwo, C. W., & Ade-Ibijola, A. (2021). Chatbots applications in education: A systematic review. *Computers and Education: Artificial Intelligence, 2,* 100033. https://doi.org/10.1016/j.caeai.2021.100033

Okubo, T., Houlden, W., Montuoro, P., Reinertsen, N., Tse, C. S., & Bastianic, T. (2023). *AI scoring for international large-scale assessments using a deep learning model and multilingual data.* Working Paper No. 287. OECD. https://one.oecd.org/document/EDU/WKP(2023)2/en/pdf

Preston, C., & Salman, J. (2024, April 11). How AI could transform the way schools test kids. *The Hechinger Report.* http://hechingerreport.org/how-ai-could-transform-the-way-schools-test-kids/

Rogers, E. M. (2003). *Diffusion of innovations* (5th ed.). Free Press.

Roose, K. (2023, January 12). Don't ban ChatGPT in schools. Teach with it. *The New York Times.* https://www.nytimes.com/2023/01/12/technology/chatgpt-schools-teachers.html

Rudolph, J., Tan, S., & Tan, S. (2023). ChatGPT: Bullshit spewer or the end of traditional assessments in higher education? *Journal of Applied Learning and Teaching, 6*(1), Article 1. https://doi.org/10.37074/jalt.2023.6.1.9

Saltman, K. J. (2022). *The alienation of fact: Digital educational privatization, AI and the false promise of bodies and numbers.* The MIT Press. ISBN 9780262544368

Sandler, R. L., Ed. (2014). *Ethics and emerging technologies.* https://doi.org/10.1057/9781137349088

Stein, S. (2024, January 17). Practical magic: VR and AR are the next big thing … again. *CNET.* https://www.cnet.com/tech/computing/practical-magic-vr-and-ar-are-the-next-big-thing-again/

Teach AI. (2023). *AI guidance for schools toolkit..* https://www.teachai.org/toolkit

UK Department of Defence. (2021). *Human augmentation—The dawn of a new paradigm.* https://assets.publishing.service.gov.uk/media/609d23c6e90e07357baa8388/Human_Augmentation_SIP_access2.pdf

Wallen, J. (2024, January 30). *4 ways Google is trying to make teachers' lives easier with AI | ZDNET.* ZDNET. https://www.zdnet.com/article/4-ways-google-is-trying-to-make-teachers-lives-easier/

Wang, X., Li, L., Tan, S. C., Yang, L., & Lei, J. (2023). Preparing for AI-enhanced education: Conceptualizing and empirically examining teachers' AI readiness. *Computers in Human Behavior, 146,* 107798. https://doi.org/10.1016/j.chb.2023.107798

Washington Office of Superintendent of Public Instruction. (n.d.). *Human centered AI in schools.* https://ospi.k12.wa.us/student-success/resources-subject-area/human-centered-artificial-intelligence-schools

WestEd. (2016). *California professional standards for education Leaders (CPSEL)*. https://www.wested.org/wp-content/uploads/2016/02/DOPS-15-03-508.pdf

Wright, M. (2023). *Personal communication.*

Xie, H., Chu, H.-C., Hwang, G.-J., & Wang, C.-C. (2019). Trends and development in technology-enhanced adaptive/personalized learning: A systematic review of journal publications from 2007 to 2017. *Computers & Education, 140*, 103599. https://doi.org/10.1016/j.compedu.2019.103599

Yang, S., & Evans, C. (2020). Opportunities and challenges in using AI chatbots in higher education. *Proceedings of the 2019 3rd International Conference on Education and E-Learning*, 79–83. https://doi.org/10.1145/3371647.3371659

Ensuring Artificial Intelligence Changes the Arc of Education for Good

Abstract This chapter expands on the changes discussed in the previous chapters and on choices surrounding AI in education that center student well-being and success. This chapter covers how educational leaders can respond to the changes that AI will bring to schools. Technology tools that employ AI models will increasingly be able to focus on student emotions in addition to knowledge generation, opening these products to difficult ethical territory. Determining the trustworthiness of AI tools lies tightly with the school administrator's range of responsibilities. By bringing in ethical frameworks, the content in this chapter explores ways leaders can think holistically about how AI can become part of an educational system that works for all students.

Keywords Artificial intelligence in education (AIED) • Emotions • Student-centered • Explainability • Trust • Privacy • Ethical leadership

This chapter expands on the changes discussed in the previous chapters and on choices surrounding AI in education that center student well-being and success. This chapter covers how educational leaders can respond to the changes that AI will bring to schools. Technology tools that employ AI models will increasingly be able to focus on student emotions as well as knowledge generation, opening these products to difficult

© The Author(s), under exclusive license to Springer Nature
Switzerland AG 2024
K. Moran Jackson, R. Papa, *AI Changing the Arc of Educational
Leadership*, https://doi.org/10.1007/978-3-031-71415-3_4

ethical territory. Determining the trustworthiness (Josephson, 2002; Marshall & Oliva, 2010) of AI tools lies tightly with the school administrator's range of responsibilities. By bringing in ethical frameworks, the content in this chapter explores ways leaders can think holistically about how AI can become part of an educational system that works for all students.

EMOTIONS: CENTERING STUDENTS AND TEACHERS

In a few words, emotions are feelings expressed along the human continuum that allow us to experience joy, sadness, fear, anger, and happiness. As educators, we understand that "identifying a student's emotional and behavioral strengths and weaknesses is critical for developing optimal learning conditions for each student" (The Center for Learning and Literacy, 2021, para. 4). AI tools have a different focus. AI applications in education usually focus on cognitive development, seeking through algorithms to "recreate" and "measure" the neurobiological human elements to assess how a student is feeling and performing.

The irrefutable reality in today's educational system is that everything must be evidence based and data driven, which limits what is being taught to only what measurement tools we use. In *The Alienation of Fact,* Saltman described the imperative for data proof schooling as having led to a situation where "social and emotional learning apps 'cure' social alienation not by engaging children in dialogue about their experiences and how their experiences are produced socially, but by putting children in front of screens to be socialized en masse by AI avatars" (Saltman, 2022, p. X). Governmental experts such as the Centers for Disease Control recommend "1-2 hours daily for children between the ages of 8 and 14" (CDC, 2023, November 1) to be on electronic devices. Understandably, the pandemic provoked drastic changes to screen time for children in schools, in defiance of the CDC recommendations on screen time.

Prior to the COVID-19 pandemic advocates for privatization such as Bill Gates called on the "end of brick and mortar schooling and the reimagining of schooling as online educations" (Saltman, 2022, p. XI) changing public education into personal learning where teaching happened with the aid of a computer software program. This call for privatization was initiated in the later quarter of the twentieth century by business roundtables with hedge fund money entering education. The movement from both political parties and at the federal government level proposed that better quantification of the curriculum would lead to improved student scores. This was the neo-liberal era where "students and parents are consumers, and knowledge as a commodity to be efficiently or inefficiently delivered" (Saltman, 2022, p. XV).

Positivism has long plagued education: the belief that learning can be rationally weighted and measured, scientifically proven with mathematical proof. Again, following the business model of industrial efficiency, Fredrick Taylor's scientific management was embraced in the early twentieth century which then led to the testing of one's intellect for entrance into universities (Taylor, 1911). Taylor was a mechanical engineer in training, which led him to see management and workers/students as productive and efficient actors that increasingly ratcheted up measurable data points. Saltman continues to see this positivism in current education reforms and stated, "knowledge and learning are delinked from both the experience of the student and from the broader social world" (Saltman, 2022, p. 9). Knowledge is separated from learning into a universal understanding that affords private industry to make a generic "one size fits all" for scalability while labeling the product as personalized. Current AI applications move us further into privatization of public education given the emphasis on personal learning and individual learning dependent on AI applications and tools.

For example, AI applications are commonly found in our homes, cars, and schools. Alexa in homes now provides music and other offerings via voice commands. Siri in cars and hand-held phones connects us with a phone, maps, music, etc. Wallach (2022) found that, as with all voice activated technology, these voice-recognition tools present privacy risks for the teacher and the student in classrooms and parents in their home. Recording is managed through continuous sensors that record all the data it hears. For example, Amazon's Echo Dot, currently in its 5th edition, has voice recognition for kids to play music, tell stories, and help with homework (St. John, 2018). This product is meant to allow kids in their own rooms to play with their AI companion and promote independent listening. It is described as follows:

> This is an experience made for younger ears. Just ask and Alexa will play music, answer questions, read stories, and tell jokes—all with kid-friendly content. In addition to the fun new design and improved speaker, you also get a 2-year worry-free guarantee and a 1-year Amazon Kids+ (FreeTime Unlimited) subscription. (Amazon, 1996–2023, p. 1)

Taken to its conclusion, Wallach noted (2022, p. 367) that "social theorists lament the emotional enrichment and lessons lost when robopets, and robo-companions are substituted for animals or people." Educators understand the known curriculum and tangible books within brick and motor schools. They also understand the need for empathy and compassion in student–teacher relationships (Peterson, 2017). Tools and applications, like this example, present unknown curriculum risks to school leaders. They will need understanding as well as plans in place that increase ethical privacy practices even with the unknown data collection happening outside of schools. Sandler described what is needed from educators and leaders this way:

> Technology continually restructures the conditions of human experience. It shapes our relationships, values, landscapes, and expectations. It alters power relationships. It makes possible new forms of life and displaces previous ones…we need to be reflective about how to develop technologies, how to incorporate them into our lives, and how to use them. That is, we need to develop frameworks and resources for evaluating emerging technologies … we need ethics and policies for emerging technologies. (Sandler, 2014, p. 23)

The flex of the AI arc is how and what algorithmic technology is measuring student cognition. Cognition and feelings are both pieces that lead to how one learns, and AI models mathematically separate them into data points for an algorithm that is based on generalizations from all students. The complexity involved is immense because the AI agent seeks to successfully bridge a "single common" algorithm while claiming it is capable of offering personalized learning. If students feel happy, it is assumed that they are in a better place to learn. Relatedly, we have learned about the negative impacts of poverty and lack of sustained food on the physiological aspects of the child. What we have not yet learned is if how a learner feels *can be measured in data* that correctly captures students' cognitive abilities.

State led efforts, along with school district leadership, are beginning to move in the direction of policy formation (discussed previously) and pragmatic guidelines regarding AI use in schools. For example, how teachers manage AI applications depends on their understanding of the limitations of AI. This next case offers insight.

Case Study #3
Part A
A middle school teacher in a rural district runs their class using a "choose your own adventure" format where students can process and demonstrate learning in different formats. Thus, different students are working on different projects throughout class time. During one afternoon, the teacher received an automated email from the school's online social studies curriculum platform, with the title "Suspected Cheating." The email was a notice that a student had been flagged while taking an online assessment. The email said, "Our AI-enhanced detection software indicates student answers had a long response time and the language pattern is indicative of other resources being consulted in answering questions."

The teacher had never seen such a report before and was unsure of the implications. The teacher was also surprised to see the report knowing the student, for whom English is their second language, to be a studious and well-meaning person. Checking the score, the assessment showed an average, if slightly high, score for the student. Further examination of the answers showed that the student had missed a few multiple-choice questions, which is typical of previous tests, but that the answers on the short-answer items were odd. Some answers had a simple structure, but other answers were more complex, although not beyond the capabilities of students who knew the material very well.

Are there ways to ethically design automatic detection systems for AI in academic use or do all systems interfere with human rights?

If these types of systems are in place who needs to be notified about the capabilities (students, parents, teachers, others, etc.) and when?

What is the role of the curriculum company versus the district in creating transparency and responsibility when enacting these AI-enabled features? What is the responsibility of the district at this point in dealing with these features?

Cheating is a very value-laden term. Davis et al. (2011) define academic cheating as "acts committed by students that deceive, mislead, or fool the teacher into thinking that the academic work submitted by the student was a student's own work" (p. 2). They also note that students who are the most emotionally invested in an outcome of an academic activity are those more likely to engage in dishonest behavior. To accuse a student of cheating is also an emotionally heavy task for teachers, as evidenced by the many posts about this circumstance to teacher social media groups and listservs. The attempt to move the burden of accusation from the teachers to a tool can be tempting. Yet, AI detection applications rely on questionable data to make their determinations. We also need to question the impact of such software on students, teachers, and the student–teacher relationship.

How teachers are advised to address AI software detection of student biometric actions has not been clearly identified in the state policies we reviewed (California, Florida, North Carolina, Texas, Virginia, and West Virginia). Most state departments of education are wrestling with generative AI but assistance is cursory in helping school administrators and teachers on how to meaningfully use AI, especially at the parent and student levels. One state, North Carolina, issued specific guidelines regarding interpreting AI detector behaviors and concluded:

> AI detectors have proven not to be dependable, therefore they should never be used as the only factor when determining if a student "cheated." Common issues with AI detectors are a high frequency of false positives for non-native English speakers and creative writers as well as a high frequency of false negatives for students who are skilled at working with AI and are capable of fooling the detectors. If there is suspicion that a student depended on AI too heavily for an assignment, this should be viewed as a teachable moment to reinforce the appropriate partnership with AI tools rather than a "gotcha" moment. Working with AI in many ways is the same as working with a tutor, asking a parent for assistance, or completing an assignment with a partner or a collaborative group. In the age of AI, it is important to focus on student reflection on the process of learning, rather than just the end product. (NCDPI, 2024, p. 24)

Underscoring this last point from North Carolina's guidelines, current approaches to curtail cheating with AI applications focus on the process. Educators can track some of the processes by scaffolding assignments, requesting outlines and drafts, tracking changes and version histories, or they can change to a product that is less susceptible to AI use, such as oral reports or in-class exams (Hernandez, 2023; Writing Across the Curriculum, 2023). Many of these process-oriented approaches also have the advantage of building a positive emotional relationship between students and teachers through sustained engagement and opportunities for feedback.

Explainability: Opening Black Boxes

When using AI applications, teacher and student interactions are critical to explaining how to arrive at a correct answer. Transactions with AI applications, such as with ChatGPT, provide both the teacher and the student the opportunity to learn about the limitations and opportunities of technology. A public urban university Technologist described interactions he has observed through the lens of his son:

> *My 13-year-old uses ChatGPT for math. His [teacher] said, I really don't care for the answer and I don't even care if you got an equation or whatever. I want you to try to figure it out. If the answer from ChatGPT, first of all, does it make sense to you? And if it doesn't, what I want you to do is go back to ChatGPT and tell them that and you explain this concept to me. So that is forced, because a student might say, give me an answer to this word problem. ChatGPT gives it to him, you write it down, you try to process it, and that's what you get. That's where you understand what ChatGPT does. But what students very seldom do is ask the same question over and over again. They don't really understand that doing that will give different answers and answers that are better in context, right within the question you're trying to ask. So, a lot of teachers are simply saying write me an essay on the intricacies of portrait photography, right? And ChatGPT comes up with this great answer. But if you were to do it again, you will know that ChatGPT has just expanded a little more. And you do that a third time and it's expanded a little more. So now, you're learning. Now you're saying, Wow, the first essay you didn't give me this, but now I know why the second essay's additional points make sense. And then you go to the third essay, and you realize what the best students are doing. That's the part where teachers and students are not understanding, the potential for that. I think this is where the potential for good AI is.* (Martinez, 2023)

The public urban university Technologist continued to focus on university faculty and teachers to gain comfort by utilizing AI in ways that will better help them understand. Understanding leads to a teacher becoming more proficient in AI use with students and self-efficacy for teaching teachers and faculty how to use it.

> *AI is not omnipresent. It's not as aware as we would expect it to be. So, when people explore certain subjects within the discipline, something in philosophy, history, you know, exploring World War Two, such as fascism, the Holocaust... AI still answers with some trepidation, right? In many [cases], it either flat out refuses to answer or, it's sort of mindful of your motives as a person. AI just says,*

"I'm not comfortable answering this question unless you explain to me why you're asking it." That's the kind of answer that really wakes up a student instantly, like, wow, okay, I see where you're going. Well, I'm asking because such and such, and then you get a whole different answer. Okay, now I get it. Let me give you the answer that I think you're looking for. And, and it's very fascinating to watch faculty do that, explore the tools that way. There are things that it flat out refuses to answer, which is kind of interesting to me, but guiding the faculty to explore so that they can learn how to co-opt it is not an easy thing to do. But it's only those faculty who are welcoming that process that end up doing well. (Martinez, 2023)

While exposure in the news and practical experiences with AI chatbots will allow teachers and students to better explain the capabilities and limitations of these applications, other AI technologies are not as easily analyzed. Equally at issue for teachers and students is the encroachment of AI biometric pedagogy used to measure student bodies (and likely faculty) through computer or iPad surveillance, including some of the wearable technologies discussed in the first chapter. The measurements are accomplished by webcam feedback devices in the software platform to "analyze changes to students' bodies in response to a lesson" (Saltman, 2022, p. 33). Saltman (2022) described the pedagogy that drives these models:

Biometric pedagogy presumes a direct, transparent, and simplistic notion of learning as depositing of knowledge … [A product] evaluates student teaching as a recorded performance that is measured by a standardized rubric. The quality and value of teaching can be read off of the body. In this case, biometric pedagogy revives behaviorist and Taylorist approaches to labor aimed at breaking down the tasks and subtasks of workers to make them increasingly approximate a continually raised targeted norm prescribed from the outset. (Saltman, 2022, pp. 33–34)

How school leaders will approach the emergent issues of advanced AI applications as described by Saltman are not easily achieved. A focus for the school leader is to ensure that the products used in the teaching and learning environment are not taken at face value from the publisher. Product transparency should reveal to school leaders how, what, and why applications are tracking information and biometrics of the students and teachers. As student biometrics are gathered and sent to the teacher for easy data management, likewise these tools are collecting teacher biometrics. The management of AI applications cannot be driven by the benefits or accuracies claimed by companies. Unproven biometric pedagogical measurements should not take over teacher-driven classroom management.

The COVID-19 pandemic ushered in AI's entrance into classrooms and allowed for the mass collection of known and unknown data gathering practices by for-profit business. The products created from the data might quickly turn into profits. Even prior to COVID-19's ubiquitous reach of technology into classrooms, gaming and social networking put students in front of screens. For example, Class Dojo, a for-profit management program found in "80% of US schools and 95% of K-8 schools, uses behavioral surveillance to levy disciplinary practices on children while inducing them to generate commercially valuable data ... treats teaching and learning physiological effects on bodies" (Saltman, 2022, p. 47). Saltman citing Jathan Sadowski, who wrote "When Data Is Capital: Datafication, Accumulation And Extraction" for the journal *Big Data and Society* (January–June, 2019, pp. 1–12), described the disparate purposes of educational AI reimagined:

> On the one hand, new educational technologies—including artificial intelligence (AI), adaptive learning, biometric pedagogy, blockchain, and the Internet of Things—are promoted by proponents as transforming the process of schooling through promises of freedom from coercion, promises of respect for student individual differences, and learning that is "personalized." These technologies measure, quantify, datafy, and normalize behavior and affect while making student activity into data manufacture. (Saltman, 2022, pp. 51–52)

Is AI leading to the rewiring of human learning being built-in to AI technology? In 2019, the World Economic Forum through crowdsourcing embarked on a description of their version of educating students titled *Education 4.0 Framework*, in concert with the Fourth Industrial Revolution (World Economic Forum: Schools of the Future, 2020). This forum identified and labeled eight characteristics as critical to both student and teacher content and their respective experiences as:

1. Global citizenship skills: Include content that focuses on building awareness about the wider world, sustainability and playing an active role in the global community.
2. Innovation and creativity skills: Include content that fosters skills required for innovation, including complex problem-solving, analytical thinking, creativity and systems analysis.

3. Technology skills: Include content that is based on developing digital skills, including programming, digital responsibility and the use of technology.
4. Interpersonal skills: Include content that focuses on interpersonal emotional intelligence, including empathy, cooperation, negotiation, leadership and social awareness.
5. Personalized and self-paced learning: Move from a system where learning is standardized, to one based on the diverse individual needs of each learner, and flexible enough to enable each learner to progress at their own pace.
6. Accessible and inclusive learning: Move from a system where learning is confined to those with access to school buildings to one in which everyone has access to learning and is therefore inclusive.
7. Problem-based and collaborative learning: Move from process-based to project- and problem-based content delivery, requiring peer collaboration and more closely mirroring the future of work.
8. Lifelong and student-driven learning: Move from a system where learning and skilling decrease over one's lifespan to one where everyone continuously improves on existing skills and acquires new ones based on their individual needs. (World Economic Forum: Schools of the Future, 2020, January, p. 4)

The World Economic Forum pedagogy framework is a combination of teaching approaches and learning principles that underpin educational systems. While many different approaches exist, literature from the World Economic Forum has emerged suggesting five key approaches for driving innovation in education systems:

1. Playful: It includes free play, guided play, and games. (The LEGO Foundation, Learning Through Play: A review of the evidence, 2018)
2. Experiential: This approach includes project-based and inquiry-based learning. (The Brookings Institution, Learning to Leapfrog: Innovative Pedagogies to Transform Education, 2019)
3. Computational: An approach that supports problem solving enabling students to understand how computers solve problems. (The Brookings Institution, Learning to Leapfrog: Innovative Pedagogies to Transform Education, 2019)
4. Embodied: An approach that incorporates the physical body into learning through movement. (OECD, Teachers as Designers of Learning Environments, 2018)

5. Multiliteracies: An approach that focuses on diversity and the multiple ways in which language is used and shared and connects learning to cultural awareness. (OECD, Teachers as Designers of Learning Environments, 2018). (World Economic Forum, 2020, p. 10)

The World Economic Forum (2020) affirmed that student learning should be reproduced in a way similar to the AI model of learning. "Teaching methods that leverage computational thinking—combining math, science and digital literacy to help students understand how to approach problems in the way that a computer would" (World Economic Forum: Schools of the Future, 2020, January, p. 9). To favor that model, in 2023 the World Economic Forum projected over the next five years that AI jobs would dramatically increase.

Personalized education originally was intended to address special needs populations in schools. Independent Educational Programs (IEPs) grew out of legislation from the 1970s. This movement when coupled with AI advancements led to a further reductive narrowing of curriculum under the guise of social-emotional learning. Yet, in the new AI-focused movement, individual student learning occurs not with student peers, but with personal interactive AI avatars. As play games move onto smartphones and tablets the human agency collective is used to "redefine play, creativity, and imagination through work and a skills-based career and technical education privatization agenda" (Saltman, 2022, p. XXI).

What actions by school administrators can ensure parents, students, and teachers about the *background data* which is collected by most AI tools? School leaders must consider the operational morality of the corporations, engineers, and programmers as the tools and applications "make no decision on their own, but merely follow the proscribed actions programmed in by designers who have predetermined all the types of situations the robot will encounter" (Wallach, 2022, p. 371). Is a single or predetermined response good for all users? For all teachers, can a single or predetermined value or norm be established? Most definitely not, at this time. A rural public school Superintendent expressed their worries:

As a district leader, it is astonishing to me the percentage of students that are digitally connected, I don't think kids have ever been more connected, in terms of digitally connected, internet, social media, etc. And yet, there's this growing percentage of kids that are suffering from isolation, being isolated, and loneliness. So, our kids are lonely, and they're isolated into digitally connected [spaces]. So, my worry is that we view these tools as a replacement for teachers. And I don't think you can replace human contact. I mean ... that shouldn't be the goal. And anything I've read on the developers of AI, that's not their intention. But I think just frankly, if we get lazy, and we think that somehow, we can just create these large labs and put one person in a lab with 70 kids, and that's going to take care of it, it's not and our children have never been [more] at risk for self-harm, drug use, and some of the other horrific things they suffer outside of school than they are now. And so, I think that's the one thing I wonder how we can use technology to make sure we can assess the student's psyche and see how they can we bring in some social emotional supports for these kids that interact in a way that surfaces, hey, this kids in crisis, they need to get help. And so, we know anecdotally, that's the case. We know a lot of our kids are in crisis. And so, we're putting more towards SEM [social-emotional] support in the form of personnel, and counselors and social workers to try to get with our kids. And what I mean by that is daily contact and try to surface those. So that's probably my other worry. (Wright, 2023)

School leaders are worried about student stress and self-harm from social media and about the use of AI in ubiquitous ways surrounding their lives. We do not advocate that school leaders need to analyze the design of algorithms or other technical requirements. We do believe that the evolving functions of AI applications mean that school leaders need to continuously revisit their own professional code of conduct and responsibly ensure that technology tools be governed by the do no harm to humanity rule. As an example discussed in Chap. 2, California has initiated a media literacy law that spans most academic subjects from kindergarten through high school to help students distinguish misinformation from disinformation.

The World Economic Forum defined education and learning based on future job projections. Education 4.0 offered a taxonomy for school learning.

The Education 4.0 Taxonomy consists of a comprehensive set of aptitudes, organized into a tree structure. Aptitudes are the abstract, transferable aspects of learning. They are teachable and learnable qualities—not innate characteristics. Most education taxonomies that pertain to childhood through secondary education identify three primary groups of aptitudes: (1) abilities and skills, (2) attitudes and values, and (3) knowledge and information ... The Education 4.0 Taxonomy places particular focus on the former two categories, as experts and employers indicate that these learning areas will require additional emphasis in future education systems relative to the emphasis they get today. (World Economic Forum, 2023, p. 7)

Aptitude is a natural or inherent ability or skill (Cambridge Dictionary, 2024). Skills are teachable. How AI addresses the complexity of natural and inherent abilities is the goal of generative AI. Who creates the data used in generative AI? Almost all of us use the Internet. Personal data has been harvested by almost every tech firm, such as websites, X, TikTok, Apple Messages, Google/Gmail, etc. (Merchant, 2023, p. A15). If this idea is not sufficiently alarming, think of the fear OpenAI marketing strategists encourage. A large urban public school district Central Office Administrator described their personal beginning:

> I remember the first time I started using some AI tools. On the one hand, I was just amazed at what it was producing. And then on the flip, there was kind of that fear. And I remember, one evening, you know, [my spouse] just kept like, going at [it], like typing things in and pulling things up. And I would joke and say, stop, stop making the singularity smarter-world [AI] because it's adapting, right. As people are searching and putting information [in], it adapts and gets better at what it does. (Nava, 2023)

OpenAI was originally a research nonprofit founded in 2015 with a large grant from Elon Musk to develop AI models and applications with responsible actions. In 2019, OpenAI's nonprofit developed for-profit limited partnerships that were meant to operate under the original nonprofit charter (Aprill et al., 2024). However, the recent drive to profit from years of development, combined with questions about the true, powerful capabilities of the models have left many to question the organization's commitment to public interest (Aprill et al., 2024). Indeed, Merchant (2023) noted that ethicists are concerned that large language models (LLMs), such as Open AI's ChatGPT, could add to the *misinformation* tunnel on the Internet due to their human-like intelligence.

What can schools do? In March of 2023, the State of Utah became "the first state to pass a law that will require users under 18 to receive consent of a parent or guardian to create social media account" and New York state is thinking of following (Ferre-Sadurni, 2023, para. 15). The harms and risks to children are increasingly at the forefront of social media. Is something similar needed for children who access AI applications as with social media applications?

AI algorithms are mathematical computations based on words they gobble up to increase their knowledge and database. With the growth of data collection in schools, is it possible for these algorithms to have enough data to not be concerned about equity, fairness, or biases? Or can these concerns become the driving force behind the algorithms? A public urban university Technologist stated their greatest concern about teacher–student interactions with AI was twofold:

> *Because AI is inherently biased (data ignores lived experiences and cultural relativity responses) it has the potential to cause many students to be accused of using AI to cheat/deceive faculty. Faculty/teachers are racing to enact policies that are restrictive/punishing and ultimately harmful to students if they aren't careful. There is no way to prove anyone is using AI, but there is also no way to prove they are not. But scared faculty/teachers are accusing students, and my guess is it will primarily affect students of color as the faculty/teacher bias is to assume they are not going to be the best writers (i.e. cultural relativity).* (Martinez, 2023)

As humans, we have not been able to achieve this without AI; therefore, can an AI application using a humongous dataset do this? Can it do so without biases? And, how will we know and trust it has our humanness in its best interest? How can we best integrate cultural norms so as to safeguard all students' well-being?

TRUST: SAFEGUARDING STUDENT PRIVACY AND WATCHING THE WATCHERS

Multiple levels of trust can be found within district policies and clearly defined practices or rules to govern the school. The evolving haste to incorporate AI in education has required teachers and administrators to reflect on how they can ensure the safety and privacy of students. How school leaders provide data governance and nondiscriminatory practices across the curriculum is difficult to account for. A school leader in the second decade of the twenty-first century cannot nor can their staff comprehend all the nuances of AI models that undergird the software programs used in schools. Thus, leaders must invest a level of trust in the programs. Without trust, school leaders would need to deeply question all decisions, such as disciplining students on the basis of AI assessments.

School leaders are constantly assessing risks as students arrive at school, during the school day in classrooms and move through the halls, or on the playground, until they return home by walking, pick-ups by parents or caregivers, or ride the school bus. The school leader knows the families that are on free-reduced breakfasts, lunches, afternoon support, and even weekend food supplements. Schools have long involved themselves in food and clothing drives for their community. The digital divide of which families and students have access to various technology tools becomes an ethical issue that school leaders must wrestle with. Global economic inequality manifests itself at the local level of families and communities. This requires the school leader to constantly access alternative approaches for accommodating differences across students, grade levels, and teachers and staff. This approach is not unlike knowing the *known* curriculum and the *unknown* curriculum. AI applications present *known* processes relating to students and teachers as well as an *unseen* data collection system with outcomes not yet known.

Case Study #3
Part B
The teacher reached out to the school tech lead, a math teacher who worked with the district office on tech initiatives and a person whom the teacher trusted. The tech lead said they had not seen that notice before either, but knew the company was making updates to their features. The tech lead came to the classroom after school and was able to pull up a more detailed activity log for the student that showed the student had opened a secondary Internet window for an online chatbot application. The teachers were not able to see what had been entered into the chatbot, but the time log showed the window open roughly at the same time as the quiz. They queried the curriculum representative for more details on the meaning of the email, but only received an automated reply that their email was received and would be processed soon. The tech lead suggested the teacher loop in the assistant principal in charge of the grade level for a meeting with the student the next day. The teacher also considered bringing in the ESL teacher who was working with the student and had been serving as an occasional assistant in class when their schedule allowed.

What are the potential benefits and concerns of bringing more adults into the conversation with the student about this incident?

In what ways is trust being tried in this incident? How should the teacher weigh their ability to trust this student versus trust their fellow teacher versus trust the AI-cheating detection software?

The West Virginia Department of Education, WVDOE (2024), published guidelines for AI use in schools. The forty-page guide offers insights into AI use, addresses the fears surrounding uses of AI, and provides the state's intention in promotion of AI tools. The WVDOE stated that generative AI "predicts the flows of language" (p. 10) with an expectation that teachers and administrators must grasp pulling from Hoffman's (2023) *Impromptu: Amplifying our Humanity Through AI*:

> While this technology does mimic human interactions, generation of ideas, and decision-making, it is important to note that as an AI "generates a reply, it is not making factual assessments or ethical distinctions about the text it is producing; it is simply making algorithmic guesses at what to compose in response to the sequence of words in your prompt." (WVDOE, 2024, p. 10)

> However, it is fundamental that realistic risks are assessed and addressed in order to protect students and staff. Predictable risks include over-reliance on AI technologies, challenges to independent and creative thinking, reduced social interactions, privacy and safety issues, furthering of digital divides, as well as plagiarism and cheating. (WVDOE, 2024, p. 10)

The North Carolina Department of Public Instruction (NCDPI) referenced the World Economic Forum Education 4.0 learning for future work as discussed earlier in this chapter. The NCDPI (2024) puts human agency at the forefront by their stated skills graduates will have developed. "North Carolina Portrait of the Graduate: adaptability, collaboration, communication, critical thinking, empathy, learner's mindset, and personal responsibility" (p. 6).

Safeguarding human agency requires informed and autonomous decisions. Who controls the algorithms, the parameters the data are employing, as well as the knowledge the programmers incorporate from their corporate headquarters, plunges the school leader into very deep water, where the known is far less than the unknown. Dealing with the unknown requires responsible constraints from school leaders for the good of their students and the teaching community.

> This powerful ability of education to shape minds—especially when it concerns young minds that are typically more malleable—can also be used to foster behaviour that might benefit developing and deploying the technology while not necessarily being in the learners' interest. More far-reaching, it can also be used to teach certain beliefs that run counter to the values of

human rights, democracy, and the rule of law and that foster instead more oppressive or totalitarian goals. (Smuha, 2022, p. 121)

An example of efforts to counteract this ability is California's media literacy law which covers most academic subjects from kindergarten through high school. Assembly Bill 873 (2023–2024) was signed into law October 2023 in direct acknowledgment of the growing reliance on technology tools. This bill intends that students understand and actively distinguish misinformation and disinformation while using social media—Internet networks. Teachers are provided media savvy professional development. The California curriculum frameworks across English, Mathematics, History-Social Science, Science, and Language Arts incorporate media literacy directly into the curriculum content at each grade level.

Smuah (2022) advocated for "strong human oversight mechanisms" (p. 122). She recommended that responsible leadership must be intentional and reliable. Reliability and reproducibility are two sides of the coin: reliability in tasks involving applied performance, and reproducibility within the same conditions of behavior. While responsibility does not solely rest on school leaders it does not entitle educators to pass blame solely on the developers.

How states/nations/school district leadership shape attitudes and tactics must be aligned with the values of human agency. Technology "requires developing an expanded conception of responsibility" (Jonas, 2014, p. 37). How school leaders learn and grow to understand the *responsible development* of the tools entering classrooms is critical. Responsible technology tools require agile policies created by curriculum experts to allow flexibility as well as safeguards. Educational leaders needs to consider carefully decisions where efficiencies may be fiscally sound, yet ultimately unethical to the school community.

Responsible Ethical Leaders

Responsible development of AI is challenging in the broadest sense: government compliance, product liability, and stakeholder intentions, often all combined with little public input in technology policy (Sandler, 2014). The rapid acceleration of AI innovation requires acknowledging "technology continually restructures the conditions of human experience. It shapes our relationships, values, landscapes, and expectations" (Sandler, 2014,

p. 23). Ethically "people who knowingly use a particular computing arti-fact are morally responsible for that use" (Wallach, 2022, p. 369). A public university Professor of Technology defines ethical thinking.

> *I think the first thing with any technologies, it comes down to ethical thinking, right? We have to help our teachers and our students and their students to really think about what the ethics are behind this. And there's lots of different ways to approach that. First of all, coming from the idea of development, why was it developed? Who's developing this? And do we want to be part of something that is being developed by this organization, because the stance of the organization is going to filter itself into the technology. Technology is always a filter of those who created it and then in AI it's a sense of those who use it and continue to its development across the way. So, I think it's really important to think of the ethics of those who have developed it, then the ethics of why am I, why are we using this? What's the importance behind us, engaging ourselves and/or our students and/ or our families in using this type of technology? If we're really using it in lim-ited capacities that could be done in any other way then what's the importance of using it? But if we're using it as a building block towards a deeper under-standing of the content that they're learning, or of how to interact with people out there in the world, or whatever it is, that becomes a really important thing.* (Armfield, 2023)

Ethical policies have a duty to value human agency over AI technology tools. The behaviors of students are governed by the rules of the school in conformance with the district policies. All ethical considerations must include if not the design or development, the deployment of desired actions through acceptable practices with students. These actions embrace the common good together with individual student behavior. The state holistically expects school leaders to keep students safe during the school day and ensure education develops the growth of the student into a knowl-edgeable, good citizen. For example, school sustainability initiatives are guided by principles of caring for one another within the school, family, community, and globally. Students learn to react in *real* time to global warming, drought conditions, violence, and other sustainability crises due to AI technological advances via *real time* technology tools. Khakurel et al. (2018) speaking about the link between AI development and sus-tainability noted that "ethics is a major consideration when making sure AI contributes to what we want. … To do this, guidance from a proper code of ethics is needed. However, developing such a 'proper' one is a significant challenge" (p. 12). A public urban university Technologist reminds us that it is okay to question and engage in reflexive thinking about our ethics.

You're going to have questions of ethics and moral compasses from your students themselves, but also from you. How do you evaluate your students on that basis, and whether you trust them enough to know that they wrote the paper? Some faculty are having this moral dilemma over things that ChatGPT will help them with to begin to write papers. (Martinez, 2023)

Questioning can also raise ethical questions as to how schools approach the responsibility of one's actions in considering the effects student actions may have on other students and the planet. It is a present question that school leaders' duty extends "farther and the anthropocentric confinement of former ethics no longer holds" (Jonas, 2014, p. 40). AI technology is an expression of our human creativity that manifests itself in the creation of tools that both aid and control our environment. These tools can lead us to deep questions about the place of compulsion and consent for learning in schools:

Shall we induce learning attitudes in school children by the mass administration of drugs, circumventing the appeal to autonomous motivation? Shall we overcome aggression by electronic pacification of brain areas? Shall we generate sensations of happiness or pleasure or at least contentment through independent stimulation (or tranquilizing) of the appropriate centers—independent, that is of the objects of happiness, pleasure, or content and their attainment in personal living and achieving? Candidacies could be multiplied. Business firms might become interested in some of these techniques for performance-increase among their employees. (Jonas, 2014, p. 44)

AI can enhance content (digitized textbooks), support students with disabilities and health impairments (virtual reality through wearable tools), and interact with students learning foreign languages (chatbots and speech recognition). Administrative tools include predicting student dropouts and real time feedback to teachers in the classrooms. The pitfalls of AI applications are also evident given their design and implementation may not have been done with real students and teachers before they were deployed. Relatedly, in an interview Sam Altman, OpenAI's CEO, said "We'll see different industries become much more productive than they used to be because they can use these tools. And that will have a positive impact on everything" (Heikkila, 2023). Educational leaders have the responsibility to question if productivity is the ultimate end goal that positively impacts everything or if there are other considerations that need to be considered.

Case Study #3
Part C

The next day, the teacher asked to speak with the student during their home room time. The teacher told the student that her assessment answers had been flagged by the software and that further investigation had revealed that a chatbot window had been opened at the same time as the assessment. The teacher then invited the student to offer an explanation.

The student explained that she had opened a chatbot that the ELA teacher had recommended in a previous class. She said that since the computer allowed her to open the chatbot, she was allowed to do so. She said she did not enter the questions from the assessment into the chatbot; she had only entered her answers. The student found that the chatbot helped her correct her grammar and use more advanced vocabulary since the online curriculum program only offered spell check for answer boxes. The student stated that although the teacher says they grade on content, that when she writes answers in better English, she believes she gets a higher score on the assessments.

After speaking with the student, what options does the teacher have for dealing with this incident? Do you believe the options have changed from before speaking with the student? Do you weigh the options differently after speaking with the student?

How does the student's explanation speak to the interplay between equality, equity, and AI access for students?

Human agency has considerations for all explanations as should AI tools in the classroom. Tools that are transparent and explainable are on the path to trustworthiness. In the case study, should the software prohibit chatbots from being opened by students? The cultural aspect of the student being an ESL student and using approved ways to clarify language is where human agency should supersede the AI tool designation. Finally, the equity issues for ESL students and for teacher practices combined with the AI tool should be thoughtfully adapted. In cases such as this, the Commonwealth of Virginia presented guiding principles for educators to safely use AI in classrooms.

- **Do no harm:** All integration of AI in education must be in accordance with the policy and IT standards that are in the Executive Order and in other state and federal policies. This includes ensuring the safeguarding of the privacy, security, and confidentiality of personally identifiable information, ensuring that algorithms are not based on inherent biases that lead to discriminatory outcomes, and that AI is only allowed when its use has the potential to contribute positive good/improvement to the status quo.

- **Prioritize integrity:** A core purpose of education is the development of responsible, ethical, and engaged citizens. Therefore, part of the integration of AI in education must be to teach about morality, ethics, honour, cheating, and how artificial intelligence can lead to perverse and destructive outcomes for individuals, relationships, and communities.

- **Augment, not replace humans:** AI cannot and should not ever replace human judgement. Although synthesis and analysis of information can be expedited through AI, it will never replace teachers who provide wisdom, context, feedback, empathy, nurturing and humanity in ways that a machine cannot. It also should not overpower/over-ride the critical thinking, judgement, and morality of the learner.

- **Harness AI to empower student success:** AI presents transformative opportunities to enrich instruction and enable more adaptive, personalized learning. To fully leverage these benefits, we must embrace an outlook of innovation and experimentation, while ensuring access for all learners. Rather than just digitizing traditional practices, we can reimagine education to nurture each student's unlimited potential with the assistive power of AI. Our vision should focus on possibility—AI as a gateway to expand human capacity—not conformity to conventions of the past.

- **Work in partnership:** AI researchers and experts in Virginia colleges and universities and employers are key partners and guides around building the skills and knowledge required to be successful in the new economy. This includes how to think about evolving AI systems and the practices needed to use them responsibly.

- **Be constantly discerning and responsive to the continuous expansion of AI capabilities and uses:** This is not a one-and-done. The guidelines, best practices, and tools available will constantly need to be revisited to keep pace with the changes brought by the exponential growth of AI and technology advancements in our world. Nimbleness and urgency, balanced with careful considerations, will be critical to ensuring we are as prepared for the continuous change ahead in education. (Commonwealth of Virginia, n.d., p. 2)

Ethics lies at the very heart of leadership. Leadership is a complex moral relationship between people, based on trust, obligation, commitment, emotion, and shared vision of the good (Ciulla, 2018). Gilligan (1982) in addition to rights and fairness included the ethic of care. The ethic of care leads us to question our definitions, for example, of plagiarism and cheating. The North Carolina Department of Public Instruction (NCDPI, 2024) described what teachers must do today.

In the not-too-distant future, it will be a common assumption that all writing from academic papers to news reports and emails may be written with AI. In light of this, it is perhaps shortsighted to automatically consider all use of AI as "cheating." Educators will need to rethink their ideas of what constitutes plagiarism and cheating in today's world, and adapt their teaching, assignments, and expectations to this new reality. (NCDPI, 2024, p. 22)

An ethical review of emerging technologies is not unlike the school leader's role with students and staff: keep everyone safe by *doing no harm*. The use of technology tools should also follow this rule. First, identifying the benefits of using technology tools, both immediate and long-term, ought to be done through student and teacher use and evaluation prior to school-wide distribution. Next, identification of the technology tools' limitations among diverse students and teachers must be promulgated.

Thinking about how this pertains to the field of education and its impacts on students and teachers is found in what is valued and thereby normed to how students are assessed (Papa & Jackson, 2022). Uncertainties are always "a precursor to sweeping change meaning that transformation is always preceded by upheaval and fear" (Brown, 2017, p. 412). Educational leaders as responsible ethical leaders work to assuage upheaval and fear so that the transformational moment benefits those in their charge.

Ethical Strategies

Ethical strategies require us to determine our ways of thinking ethically. When dealing with AI applications, school leaders need to help our teachers and students to think about the ethics of use: what are the different ways to approach content? If an AI application is chosen, the school leader must consider why it was developed and what it was developed for. The positioning of the school policy filters itself through its AI use. How do we use that technology? How do we prepare people to think about those technologies? How do we make sure it is going to be used in a way that is not harmful to anyone? And how does AI predict growth?

Real judgment should be used when educators are assigning students to use AI applications while clearly understanding expectations of student use. AI applications can magnify human biases, biases hidden from the awareness of users (Beckner, 2004; Garcia, 2016; Turk, 2023). Instead of banning AI applications from classrooms, the more teachers understand AI, the more the tools can be used to guide students to a deeper understanding of the content being delivered. A public urban university Technologist explained how individual biases are magnified through AI.

> [Teachers] exercise some real judgment, I think, where you have a little more control over why you're assigning [content] to students and what you're expecting from students. You know, in many ways, I think this magnifies small little biases we had before. ... I mean, [teachers] all have biases, but this thing [AI] has really magnified them because it's made people less aware of what the potential is and does. They [teachers] don't know the possibilities. I think they're more afraid of it, and therefore magnifying their own insecurity bias, in terms of what their students can and should be able to accomplish with tools like this. And I think some faculty are doing good. I think some faculty are doing excellent in how they manage it. But a lot more than not are not doing so well. (Martinez, 2023)

Ethical strategies require the educational leader to actualize ethical actions in their practices. For ethical leaders the law is the floor we metaphorically stand on. We know that because something is not illegal does not mean it is right. The ethical world is messy and complex. Prior to being able to access the Internet we could base our decisions as leaders on available, local data. AI tools bring a very different approach as the data itself may be hidden and the decision-making process may not be based on moral ethical guides that serve students and teachers. Kohlberg (1969) drew upon conflict as moral issues centering on individual rights and fairness. In this book we have made parts of cases intertwined with ideas to aid in a leader's guidance. In the resolution of conflict, objectivity must be questioned in consideration of AI tools, just as power and privilege must be found on principles of ethics to remain at the heart of human agency.

AI posthumanism (Bostrom, 2017) foretold three levels that increase in distinguished complexity based on "a general central capacity greatly exceeding the maximum attainable by any current human being without recourse to new technological means" (p. 219). The first level of capacity is healthcare, as humans desire to live healthier longer for *extra life* . How life is improved in old age or even how the aging processes are delayed has been a part of medical practices since the turn of the twenty-first century. The second level of post-humanist capacity is optimizing cognition and intellectual performance. What is now found in AI tools in classrooms, though in its infancy, may instigate personal reliance on AI to achieve greater cognition, such as "enhancing abstract reasoning ability" (p. 225). The third posthuman capacity is emotional enhancement and is considerably more difficult. "It is difficult to understand what such novel emotions and mental states might be like. This is unsurprising, since by assumption we currently lack the required neurological bases" (p. 226). A public urban university Technologist who works with faculty across disciplines to induct AI into their classrooms described the post human capacity:

> But more importantly faculty are scared of what may happen in five years with the amount of knowledge this AI ... is carrying right now in the amount of questions and information and ... I'm not sure I will call it ... sentient and feeling. It has feelings and emotions, but the way to respond to it [acknowledges] students like it right. It sure seems like it's getting some madness coming out of it. (Martinez, 2023)

Educational leaders can question if emotional enhancements to one's emotions, such as happiness or depression, support human agency in our relationship with AI. Are we not already experiencing crossover with health and cognition in classrooms? Increasingly AI tools support special needs that are both cognitive and emotional. Educational leaders' awareness of the potential results of AI applications is exceedingly worthwhile. Ethics for educational leaders can be divided into five frames:

Ethic of Justice	Rule of law, justice, equity If a law/policy is silent does that mean it is ethical? Should AI applications be taken at face value that they are safe for all students? How has the AI tool been responsibly developed?
Ethic of Critique	Social class inequities How are student differences—emotionally, physically, culturally—considered in AI software? Is there enough transparency with the AI tool that can assure educators of its protections? Who is empowered and who is disempowered by technology?
Ethic of Care	Harm/benefit—What are the long-term effects of decisions? How can we assure parents their child is not harmed by using AI? How can we assure parents their child is benefitting from AI?
Ethic of Community	Commit to share our stories, respect all views and values of others. What assurances does the software provide that demonstrate respect for students? Respect for parents? Respect for teachers?
Ethic of Profession	Commit to ethical leadership—Are you inspiring to others? Educational Leaders who are ethical commit to strategies: Identifying how technology restructures classroom activities Identifying how technology affects the individual Identifying the social implications Identifying the ecological conditions of students, parents, teachers Identifying alternative approaches not using technology

Over a decade ago, Wallach (2022) identified moral responsibilities for "the design, development, or deployment of computing artifacts" (p. 369). Two of the four rules can be applied to the ethics of a school administrator. "Rule 3: People who knowingly use a particular computing artifact are morally responsible for that use" (p. 369). Applying this rule in education would include students, parents, teachers, staff, and community leaders. "Rule 4: People who knowingly design, deploy, or use a computing artifact can do so responsibly only when they make a reasonable effort to take into account the sociotechnical systems in which the artifact is embedded" (p. 369). Consider a game avatar that has been built with sensors that can discern distress from the child, or the newest model of a car built with sensors of eye movements that detect when the driver's eyes are not directly looking forward. Biometrics and neurological AI capabilities are likely not suitable for all users. A public university Professor of Technology reminds us:

> We don't use technology to do the same things that we've always done. We use technology to better ourselves as individuals as a society. And finally, thinking about ethics is what are the potential benefits and downfalls we always need to be thinking about? What's the good in this? What's bad in this? And how do we limit the things that we don't want? And how do we increase the things that we do want? And so those are really important things we want. We want teachers always thinking about that as we want students always thinking about that, because that's how we become better as people, and that's how we interact and how we connect as people. (Armfield, 2023)

POTENTIAL: ASKING THE RIGHT QUESTIONS

Albert Einstein told us to "learn from yesterday, live for today, hope for tomorrow. The important thing is not to stop questioning" (Brainy Quote, 2024–2001, p. 1). The basic ethical principle of **do no harm** is at the heart of all schooling policies and practices, including AI tools. Ethical questions to ask: Who benefits from the decision/action? Who is potentially harmed by the decision/action? How can the school leader mitigate the harm? Who is silenced?

Questions of AI tool usage might include: Are student prompts adaptable to meet the diversity of students? Are technology tools able to be reconfigured to meet the teacher and student needs? Of major concern are issues of student and teacher privacy. Is surveillance of students good if it can detect a gun in a student's backpack?

What is the potential for good AI in educational spaces? Exploring the potential for good necessitates transparency in how to use AI applications. Educators and students should be able to explain how they wrote the paper or answered the equation. Does it make sense to ask about the right questions given the speed of rapid transition due to AI at this time in the twenty-first century? Yet, formulating our thoughts into questions is necessary especially for pre-K-12 educators. All questions can have a practical and common-sense basis when at the heart of them is the well-being of students. A public university Professor of Technology who teaches future teachers and administrators how best to survive in the school setting pondered:

It has to be about looking at the technology for what it is and really understanding, is it providing consistent feedback? Even as we use the tool it's growing, right, even as it's changing, because we know that it's going to change and the input that we put into an AI system modifies that system. Is it staying consistent over time? Is it? Is it helping us to expand on ideas or not? And I think that that's got to be the future of it. It can't just be the simple feedback loop. It has to be this loop that says, "Hey, you're there. How do we get here?" Those are great conversations to have with your teachers in the classroom…How do we use that technology? Or how do we need to prepare people to think about those technologies? Not just in that critical sense, but why am I using it? When am I using it? Who's going to use it? How do we make sure that it's going to be used in a way that is not harmful to anyone? And, you know, and that predicts growth? (Armfield, 2023)

References

Aprill, E., Chan Loui, R., & Horwitz, J. R. (2024). Board control of a charity's subsidiaries: The saga of OpenAI. *Tax Notes Federal, Volume 182*, UCLA School of Law, Law-Econ Research Paper No. 24-01, Loyola Law School, Los Angeles Legal Studies Research Paper No. 2024-04. https://papers.ssrn.com/sol3/papers.cfm?abstract_id=4720202

Armfield, S. (2023). *Personal communication.*

Assembly Bill No. 873 California State. (2023–2024). *Assembly Bill No. 873 Pupil instruction: Media literacy: Curriculum frameworks, Berman.* https://leginfo.legislature.ca.gov/faces/billTextClient.xhtml?bill_id=202320240AB873

Beckner, W. (2004). *Ethics for educational leaders*. Pearson. ISBN: 0-205-360091-2

Bostrom, N. (2017). *Superintelligence: Paths, dangers, strategies*. Oxford. ISBN 978-0-19-873983-8

Brainy Quote. (2024–2001). *Albert Einstein*. https://www.brainyquote.com/search_results?x=0&y=0&q=albert+einstein

Brown, D. (2017). *Origin*. Doubleday. ISBN 978038551423

Cambridge Dictionary. (2024). *Aptitude*. https://dictionary.cambridge.org/us/dictionary/english/aptitude

CDC, Center for Disease Control. (2023, November 1). *Screen Time vs. Lean Time Infographic.*. https://archive.cdc.gov/www_cdc_gov/nccdphp/dnpao/multimedia/infographics/getmoving.html.

Ciulla, J. B. (2018). Ethics and effectiveness: The nature of good leadership. In J. Antonakis & D. Day (Eds.), *The nature of leadership* (3rd ed., pp. 439–467). Sage. ISBN: 9781483359274.

Commonwealth of Virginia. (n.d.). Guidelines for AI integration throughout education in the Commonwealth of Virginia. https://www.education.virginia.gov/media/governorvirginiagov/secretary-of-education/pdf/AI-Education-Guidelines.pdf

Davis, S. F., Drinan, P. F., & Gallant, T. B. (2011). *Cheating in school: What we know and what we can do*. John Wiley & Sons.

Ferre-Sadurni, L. (2023, October 13). New York seeks to free children from algorithms. *New York Times, Business,* para. 15.

Garcia, M. (2016). Racist in the machine: The disturbing implications of algorithmic bias. *World Policy Journal, 33*(4), 111–117.

Gilligan, C. (1982). *In a different voice: Psychological theory and women's development*. Harvard University Press.

Heikkila, M. (2023, April 10). AI literacy might be ChatGPT's biggest lesson for schools. *MIT Technology Review*. https://mailchi.mp/technologyreview.com/ai-literacy-chatgpt-biggest-lesson-for-schools?e=d224bd8ec1

Hernandez, M. (2023, February 8). AI-resistant assignments? Show student thinking and promote better writing with UChicago-supported tools. *Academic Technology Solutions, University of Chicago*. https://academictech.uchicago.edu/2023/02/08/ai-resistant-assignments-show-student-thinking-and-promote-better-writing-with-uchicago-supported-tools/

Hoffman, R. (2023). *Impromptu: Amplifying our humanity through AI*. Dallepedia. ISBN: 979-8-9878319-1-5

Jonas, H. (2014). Technology and responsibility: Reflections on the new tasks of ethics. In R. L. Sandler (Ed.), *Ethics and emerging technologies* (pp. 37–47). Palgrave Macmillan. https://doi.org/10.1057/9781137349088

Josephson, M. (2002). *Making ethical decisions: The basic primer on using the six pillars of character to make better decisions and a better life*. Josephson Institute of Ethics. ISBN: 1-888869-13-7

Khakurel, J., Penzenstadler, B., Porras, J., Knutas, A., & Zhang, W. (2018). The rise of artificial intelligence under the lens of sustainability. *Technologies, 6*(4), Article 4. https://doi.org/10.3390/technologies6040100

Kohlberg, L. (1969). Stage and sequence: The cognitive development approach to socialization. In D. Goslin (Ed.), *The handbook of socialization theory and research* (pp. 347–480). Rand McNally.

Marshall, C., & Oliva, M. (2010). *Leadership for social justice*, 2nd ed. Allyn & Bacon. ISBN-13: 978-0-13-136266-6

Martinez, M. (2023). *Personal communication.*

Merchant, B. (2023, August 26). Business: Who's helping train AI? Almost all of us. *Los Angeles Times*, A15.

Nava, M. (2023). *Personal communication.*

NCDPI-North Carolina Department of Public Instruction. (2024, January 16). *North Carolina generative AI implementation recommendations and considerations for pk-13 public schools.* https://www.ednc.org/wp-content/uploads/2024/03/NCDPI-Generative-AI-Implementation-Recommendations-and-Considerations-for-PK-13-Public-Schools-v.24.02_385744pdiosjzimpplqnpoo3zdyqyz.pdf

Papa, R., & Jackson, K. M. (Eds.). (2022). *Artificial intelligence, human agency and the educational leader.* Springer. https://doi.org/10.1007/978-3-030-77610-7

Peterson, A. (2017). *Compassion and education: Cultivating compassionate children, schools and communities.* Palgrave. https://doi.org/10.1057/978-1-137-54838-2

Saltman, K. J. (2022). *The alienation of fact: Digital educational privatization, AI and the false promise of bodies and numbers.* The MIT Press. ISBN 9780262544368.

Sandler, R. L. (Ed.). (2014). *Ethics and emerging technologies.* https://doi.org/10.1057/9781137349088

Smuha, N. A. (2022). Pitfalls and pathways for trustworthy artificial intelligence in education. In W. Holmes & K. Porayska-Pomsta (Eds.), *The ethics of artificial intelligence in education* (pp. 113–145). Routledge.

St. John, A. (2018, April 26). What parents need to know about the Amazon Echo Dot Kids Edition. *Consumer Reports.* https://www.consumerreports.org/smart-speakers/amazon-echo-dot-kids-edition-what-parents-need-to-know/

Taylor, F. (1911). *The principles of scientific management.* Harper and Brothers.

The Center for Learning and Literacy. (2021). *Emotional functioning and behavior..* https://mycll.org/for-parents-and-teachers/emotional-functioning-and-behavior/

The Lego Foundation. (2018). *Learning through play: Strengthening learning through play in early childhood education programmes.* UNICEF. https://www.unicef.org/sites/default/files/2018-12/UNICEF-Lego-Foundation-Learning-through-Play.pdf

Turk, V. (2023, October 10). *How AI reduces the world to stereotypes*. Rest of World. https://restofworld.org/2023/ai-image-stereotypes/

Wallach, W. (2022). Ethics, law, and governance in the development of robots. In R. L. Sandler (Ed.), *Ethics and emerging technologies* (pp. 363-379). Palgrave Macmillan. https://doi.org/10.1057/9781137349088 ISBN 978-0-230-367349088

World Economic Forum. (2020). *Schools of the future: Defining new models of education for the fourth industrial revolution* (pp. 1–34). https://www.weforum.org/publications/schools-of-the-future-defining-new-models-of-education-for-the-fourth-industrial-revolution/

World Economic Forum. (2023, January). *Defining education 4.0: A taxonomy for the future of learning*. https://www3.weforum.org/docs/WEF_Defining_Education_4.0_2023.pdf

Wright, M. (2023). *Personal communication*.

Writing Across the Curriculum. (2023, Winter). *AI-resistant assignments*. Carleton College. https://www.carleton.edu/writing/resources-for-faculty/working-with-ai/ai-resistant-assignments/

WVDOE-West Virginia Department of Education. (2024, January). *Guidance, considerations, & intentions for the use of artificial intelligence in West Virginia schools*. https://wvde.us/wp-content/uploads/2024/03/30438-WVDE-AI-Guidance-v1.pdf

CHAPTER 5

Conclusion

Abstract In this book, we discussed how artificial intelligence (AI) is changing the arc of education. AI applications are changing the work of students, teachers, and educational leaders. These changes are raising wicked questions, forcing educators to wrestle with how to remain ethical and student-centered while using these new tools. AI is changing how education is thought about, delivered, and received. It is changing the lived experiences of students, educators, and administrators alike. It is changing how teachers are trained and how students learn. AI has and continues to change the arc of education.

Keywords Artificial intelligence in education (AIED) • Ethical leadership • Student-centered education • Wicked problems

In this book we have offered a myriad of thoughts, positive, neutral, and harmful for the educational leader to learn about how artificial intelligence is changing the arc of education. AI curricular tools manifest rapid complex rethinking of how schools and universities handle data processes and natural language processing. We have labeled our questions raised in this book as wicked questions implying there is no one answer nor situation for which to seek best practices. Wicked questions are forcing educators to wrestle with how to remain student centered.

K. Moran Jackson, R. Papa, *AI Changing the Arc of Educational Leadership*, https://doi.org/10.1007/978-3-031-71415-3_5

How educators are learning to live and work with artificial intelligence raises many wicked questions about ethics, educational principles, roles, and responsibilities. These wicked questions are appearing across educational landscapes as we encounter this new technology in new ways. AI is changing how education is thought about, delivered, and received. It is changing the lived experiences of students, educators, and administrators alike. It is changing how teachers are trained and how students learn. Without the COVID-19 pandemic and the introduction of AI in education (AIED) within the last decade, it would be hard to argue that education would look the same now as we thought it would look before these major societal and technological disruptions. AI has and continues to change the arc of education.

Understanding how educational leaders respond to AIED change requires awareness to intentionally develop ones' spidey senses, ensuring that the face value from those developing and selling AIED products are trustworthy. We addressed ethical strategies as a moral compass for the educational leader to understand how transparency and modifiability ensures the variety of students are having their needs met.

Change is ubiquitous as AI enters the lives of students and teachers necessitating each wicked problem in relationship to other problems: seeking unique solutions for the unique students in front of us. The twentieth century notably focused on "best practices" which devolves into static thinking and practices that seek replicability. AIED is not and should not be considered as best in practice. It may be sold to districts and universities as "best" but this thinking does not reflect our understanding of AI.

While the path of education has veered increasingly toward student-centered practices (Kliebard, 2004), technology has not always taken the same path in becoming more person-centered. The economic push for profitable applications means that much of what we are seeing is corporation-centered, not student-centered. While many AI theorists, most notably Shneiderman (2022) and Holmes and Porayska-Pomsta (2023), have called for AI that centers humans and their educational experiences, there remain many problems with how AI is being implemented in schools and society. The overflow of policy documents from professional organizations and government agencies reflects how systems are attempting to push back against the tide of AI applications that are bending our educational practices.

While AI applications were originally touted, and continue to be touted, as solutions to educational problems, we are realizing that these tools only perpetuate older wicked problems in education. There continues to be discussions about equal distributions of resources, how and if educational efficacy can be measured, and the perpetuation of social bias in educational systems, among a myriad of other problems. What we would like readers to recognize is that there is not likely to ever be a simple solution. AI will not solve our problems. Although it might ameliorate some of them, it will raise others.

We must always ask, Who benefits? And Who is harmed? in order to contest easy solutions. Commonality of practices asks us to address wicked questions in order to learn how best and when best use of AIED should be utilized by students. The arc of education is continually challenging how we learn: this involves a laser sharp single-mindedness on student well-being. These are exciting times for educational leaders to navigate.

REFERENCES

Holmes, W., & Porayska-Pomsta, K. (Eds.). (2023). *The ethics of artificial intelligence in education: Practices, challenges, and debates.* Routledge. https://doi.org/10.4324/9780429329067

Kliebard, H. M. (2004). *The struggle for the American curriculum, 1893–1958* (3rd ed.). Routledge.

Shneiderman, B. (2022). *Human-centered AI.* Oxford. https://doi.org/10.1093/oso/9780192845290.001.0001

INDEX

A

Access, 15, 17, 18, 20, 23, 35, 36, 38, 41, 44, 55, 70, 73, 75, 80, 81, 83

Accessibility, 36–38

Administration, 2, 49, 52, 79

Agency (human agency), 54, 71, 76–78, 80, 84, 92

See also Autonomy

Algorithm (data), 1, 9, 22, 23, 39, 62, 64, 72–74, 76, 81

See also Data

Artificial intelligence (AI), v, vi, 1–4, 7–27, 33–56, 61–87, 91, 92

agent, 23, 64

applications, 2, 8, 9, 12, 13, 17–20, 22–26, 33–36, 38, 40–46, 53, 62–64, 66–68, 72–75, 79, 83–85, 87, 92

literacy, 19, 71

Artificial intelligence in education (AIED), v, 17, 19, 92, 93

Assessment (tests/testing/grading), 5, 9, 13, 24–26, 34–40, 42, 44, 50, 52, 54, 55, 65, 74, 76, 80

Attitudes, 16, 17, 19, 72, 77, 79

See also Perceptions

Autonomy, 12–15, 26, 43, 44

See also Agency

B

Ban, 43

See also Policy

Benefits, 12, 25–27, 44, 45, 49, 51, 68, 75, 76, 81, 82, 85, 86, 93

Bias, 20, 21, 23, 74, 83, 93

Biometrics, 66, 68, 69, 86

C

Chatbot, 22, 34–36, 40, 68, 75, 79, 80

ChatGPT, 11–13, 24, 40, 41, 52, 53, 67, 73, 79

Cheating, 9, 34, 53, 65, 66, 76, 81, 82

Collaborative learning (collaborative work), 9, 10, 26, 70

Content knowledge, 11, 13, 39, 40
Coronavirus disease (COVID-19), 9,
    53, 62, 69, 92
Creativity, 10, 44, 69, 71, 79
Curriculum, 10, 11, 39, 43, 45–47,
    49–51, 55, 63–65, 71, 74,
    75, 77, 80

D
Data (database/data collection/
    background data), 2, 3, 11,
    19–24, 27, 34, 35, 37, 39,
    62–64, 66, 68, 69, 71,
    73–76, 83, 91
Deepfakes, 25
Diversity, 23, 48, 71, 86

E
Education, v, 1–4, 8–10, 14, 16, 17,
    20, 22, 33–56, 61–87, 91–93
Educational institutions (educational
    organizations), vi, 38, 44, 48, 49
Educational leaders, v, 3, 4, 14–16,
    26, 33, 34, 43, 46–49, 61, 77,
    79, 82–84, 91–93
Educational technology (ed-tech), 9,
    10, 16, 17, 53, 69
Educators, 2–5, 8–10, 12, 16–19, 21,
    22, 25, 26, 35–39, 41, 43–46,
    49–51, 62, 64, 66, 77, 80, 82,
    83, 85, 87, 91, 92
Efficacy (self-efficacy), v, 16, 33, 35,
    45–46, 67, 93
Emotions, 45, 61–66, 82, 84
Equity, 36, 48, 55, 74, 80, 85
Ethical leadership, 85
Ethical strategies (ethical actions),
    49–51, 83–86, 92
Explainability, 67–74

F
Florida, 49, 51, 66

G
Generative AI, 11, 20, 25, 34–36, 38,
    66, 73, 76
Google, 35–37, 40, 73
Guidelines, 12, 14, 53, 64, 66,
    76, 81

H
Hallucinations, 25
Harms, 12, 20–25, 44, 72, 73,
    81, 82, 86
Health, 37, 54, 79, 84

I
Illinois, 49, 50
Inequality, 17, 18, 20, 50, 75
Instruction, 16, 46, 50, 81
International Society for Technology
    in Education (ISTE), 51
Internet, 71, 73, 75, 77, 83
    See also Online

J
Justice, 48, 85

L
Large language models (LLMs),
    24, 25, 73
    See also Chatbot; Generative AI
Laws, 22, 25, 47–49, 51, 54, 72, 73,
    77, 83, 85
Leadership, 45, 47–49, 51, 64, 70,
    77, 82, 85

Learning, 2, 8–11, 13, 15, 19, 23, 26,
    34, 35, 37, 38, 41, 43, 44,
    48–51, 53–55, 62–72, 76,
    79, 81, 92
Lesson plans (lesson planning), 26,
    34, 36, 45

M
Machine learning, 9, 13, 39
Misinformation, 54, 72, 73, 77
Motivation, 26, 46, 79

N
National Policy Board for Educational
    Administration (NPBEA),
    14, 47–49
Natural language processing
    (NLP), 2, 11, 24, 34, 85,
    86, 91
Networks, 23, 54, 77
Neural networks, 24
North Carolina, 66

O
Online, 9, 10, 54, 55, 62, 65,
    75, 80
OpenAI, 73, 79
Organisation for Economic
    Co-operation and Development
    (OECD), 70, 71

P
Parents, v, 4, 16–21, 27, 41, 42, 46,
    53–56, 63, 66, 71, 73, 74, 85
Pedagogy, 68–70
Perceptions, 1, 11, 12, 19, 56
    See also Attitudes

Personalization (personalized
    learning), 10, 12, 26, 34,
    35, 37, 39
Policy, 19, 20, 25, 34, 41, 43, 44, 47,
    48, 50–56, 63, 64, 66, 74, 77,
    78, 81, 83, 85, 86, 92
    See also Laws
Privacy, v, 2, 15, 18, 21, 22, 35, 36,
    74–77, 81, 87
Professional development, 12, 14, 35,
    45, 48, 49, 52, 55, 77
Professional standards (professional
    codes), 47–50, 72

R
Recommendations, 7, 8, 43, 62
Relationships, 17, 23, 48, 50, 64, 66,
    77, 81, 82, 84, 92
Responsible leadership, 77
Rights, 18, 26, 37, 39, 40, 45, 47, 52,
    53, 55, 65, 67, 73, 77, 78,
    82–84, 87
Risk, v, 15, 20, 21, 23, 25–27, 54, 63,
    64, 72–74, 76

S
Social-emotional, 44, 48, 50,
    51, 71, 72
Social expectations, 19, 44
Social media, 17–19, 34, 54, 66,
    71–73, 77
Software, 1, 9, 15, 16, 21, 24, 34, 36,
    62, 65, 66, 68, 74, 75, 80, 85
Stereotypes, 23
Student, v, 2, 4, 8–13, 15–17, 20–22,
    25–27, 34–56, 61–72,
    74–87, 91–93
Student-centered, 92
Sustainability, 69, 78

T

Teachers, v, 9, 10, 12–17, 19–21, 25–27, 34–36, 38, 41–47, 50, 52, 55, 56, 62–69, 71, 72, 74–83, 85–87, 92

Teaching, 2, 10, 13–16, 18, 26, 34–38, 41, 44, 46, 47, 49–51, 62, 67–71, 76, 82

Theory, 8, 12, 39, 45

Transformer models, 24

Transparency, 48, 65, 68, 85, 87, 92

Trust, 15, 48, 74–77, 79, 82

20th century, 62, 92

21st century, 10, 15, 44, 47, 87

U

United Nations Children's Fund (UNICEF), 8

V

Virginia (Commonwealth of Virginia), 54, 66, 80–82

Virtual reality (VR or XR), 36, 37, 79

See also Wearable technology

W

Washington State, 54

Wearable technology, 36, 68

See also Virtual reality

Well-being, 47, 48, 55, 61, 74, 87, 93

West Virginia, 66

Wicked problems, 3–6, 18, 25, 52, 92, 93

World Economic Forum, 69–72, 76

GPSR Compliance

The European Union's (EU) General Product Safety Regulation (GPSR) is a set of rules that requires consumer products to be safe and our obligations to ensure this.

If you have any concerns about our products, you can contact us on

ProductSafety@springernature.com

In case Publisher is established outside the EU, the EU authorized representative is:

Springer Nature Customer Service Center GmbH
Europaplatz 3
69115 Heidelberg, Germany